Rocks & Butterflies

Rocks & Butterflies

"KIEBA" DAWN BLACKLIDGE

Rocks & Butterflies is a Conscious Shift Publication

Conscious Shift Publishing Registered Offices: 1700 66th St N #104-225 Saint Petersburg, FL 33710

Library of Congress Control Number: 2017961464

Dawn Erica Blacklidge

Rocks & Butterflies

ISBN: 9780997955262
ISBN : 0997955260

Dawn Erica Blacklidge

Published in the United States of America

Book design by Ellen Kaltenbacher

While the author made every effort to provide accurate information at the time of publication, neither the publisher nor the author assumes any responsibility for errors, or for changes that may occur after publication.

This book is creative nonfiction. The information and events in this book are the memories of the author. The events have been expressed and written as remembered by the author. Names and identifying details have been changed to protect the privacy of individuals.

Dedication

I dedicate this book of my life's journey to:
Everyone who helped me find my jaded dull rocks and polish them
to shiny, smooth beauties.
Everyone who threw sharp, hurtful rocks at me so that I would learn
to dodge them.
Everyone who helped me find those caterpillars so I could watch
their metamorphosis as they became butterflies and flew from their
safe haven.
Everyone who captured, caged, or clipped the wings of my butterflies
to teach me to grow new wings, or find a way out to fly free from hurt.
Especially, to those family members and friends who have always
shown unconditional love and support, throughout my life.
And, special thanks to those that physically contributed to the writ-
ing of this book...
Selene Wallace your creativity helped bring life to my story.
Also, my editor: Melanie Blenis, my friends, and photographers:
Sean King, Rhiannon Cloud and Abby Laden. And I extend heart-
felt thanks to Elizabeth Kekedi for believing in me and this project.
All of you are treasures.
And thanks to my ever faithful, four-legged, companion, Austi girl,
for licking away my tears as I wrote.

Breath-Believe-Receive. And, anyone can FLY.

Table of Contents

Prologue

This book has very little to do with the geology of rocks or the biology of butterflies other than realizing potential when there seems to be none. Mundane, unpolished rocks can be tossed into a tumbler to come out days later, as dusty treasures, ready to be shined and admired. Butterflies are bent to the will of the wind, yet when they land on a flower to collect nectar, they are one of the most beautiful, hardest workers on the earth. Though either may be easily disregarded upon first look, they perform duties that are a vital part of the whole ecosystem by being minerals, metals or transporters of a life source. Rocks and butterflies also fulfill needs, as a part of a spiritual realm, offering elemental strength and natural beauty when we are open to receive them.

When applied to my life, rocks and butterflies have always been around. Early on, there were rock collecting days with my family, and now there are thoughts of my grandmother with every butterfly I see. We all have those pits in our stomachs when things aren't quite right, and our spirits soar when we've stayed true to ourselves. Each rock and flight path symbolize a situation in our lives. This book is my collection, laid open for you.

I hope to show how much we can falter, lose hope, get beaten down, and still look to tomorrow as a new day. We all carry the boulders of our past with us. I've learned that allowing the guilt or regret or sadness to weigh me down interferes with the potential I have. Looking at the processes that made such a rock can reveal how to unravel its hold, so I can put it away and better understand if ever there is a next time.

The same applies for every time our feet don't hit the ground because of an accomplishment, a compliment, a love realized, a feeling of absolute contentment. If I analyze the rise, I may be able to do it again. When I feel an upswing, even if I'm in a slump, I know there's purpose in my life. By listening to my gut and learning from both bad and good, I can look up on my shelf of maturity, and see it filled with beauty, shine, and sparkle rather than uncut, unrealized, or torn wishes.

I particularly want to reach out to women who know there's more inside of them but feel they're stuck. Sometimes, we get into situations for a greater good, but it turns out neither good nor great. To make life easier, we may conform ourselves to someone we're not meant to be. By telling my story, I hope to give a spark of action to those who yearn for fulfillment but need a bolster of self-confidence. No more *maybe someday*, or *I wish I could*, but rather: *anything is possible*, and *everything is doable*.

Throughout the years, I've heeded to my inner voice despite any outside negativity, and it's led me to an amazing life of doing what I love. It may not be the path you would have chosen, but the situations I've encountered may ring true. It's my lessons that I hope will help others. We can choose. The choices we make define our life. I choose happiness and love, passion, and progress.

PART ONE

Going With My Gut

The trophy had lights as bright as Christmas.
It was my fourth bodybuilding competition, and I had just
won first place!
My seven-year-old daughter ran up on stage, and we shot matching
smiles and
bicep poses for the cameras.
It was one of the best days of my life.
I had done it all my way.

Taking Risks

When I was eight, I left fear behind. I stood at the edge of the highest diving board at the Kokomo Country Club and looked down at the water far below. The height was dizzying. My heart raced so hard my stomach became a punching bag. Breathing became claustrophobic, and I looked at the ladder leading the way back down. For a millisecond that took a million years, everything just stopped. Though my feet felt as if they were rooted to the spot, I could still see myself in the air. I was paralyzed yet knew that other people jumped so I could, too. I closed my eyes and filled my lungs with courage, pumped my legs, and took off flying. In those next screaming moments, I knew I could do anything as long as I told myself I could. A life with a little fear is better than wasting opportunities just because they are tough or frightening or even out of the norm.

Just over twenty years later, I was a single mother stuck in a rut. There were things in my life that I adored. My daughter, Autumn, was six and the light of my life. Being just the two of us brought many hardships, but I'd fought for her, and I wouldn't have it any other way. My pregnancy was rough, and being married to her father wasn't planned nor did it turn out to be forever, but Autumn made my soul fly above the clouds.

I truly loved my job. Fitness, health, and wellness had always been important to me, but when I'd started going to the gym and working out, it had awakened a burning passion. I'd dug deep for a year, earned my trainer's certification and had recently become the new Fitness Director at the Kokomo Sports Center. Sharing my knowledge as a trainer satisfied many desires in my life.

I was also training for bodybuilding competitions. After nine months of consistent attendance of bodybuilding, fitness, and strength training classes at the gym, I'd been encouraged to enter into a competition. Three months of absolute dedication had gained me third place in the Indiana State Championship competition. I was enamored being able to see the difference in my body because of my hard work.

Despite these things, I felt a stagnancy. I was born Dawn Erica Blacklidge, first child and first grandchild in a family that owned the successful *Kokomo Tribune* newspaper in 1959. Three more children came along to make our unit three girls and three boys with a close relationship to both sets of grandparents. Though any actual pressure was rare, I always felt an expectation to set a good example for my siblings and represent the family well. We were quite active together, taking many trips near and far, spending summers at our lake house in Culver and cheering each other on in whatever sport was in season. For me, Kokomo was always comfortable since our family bond had been tight. Throughout my life, I'd still go back, but, in recent years, its allure was fading. I felt I was growing in ways that were not comfortable for Kokomo.

In June of 1989, my daughter flew to California for two weeks to visit her father and his girlfriend. The first week, she called crying every day. Quite understandably, her father was trying to get to know her, and she felt like she was staying with a stranger. I decided to fly over for the second week in hopes to save a few tears and feelings of rejection.

Since I was only months away from competing in my second bodybuilding competition, I found a gym nearby so I could continue to train. The tanned, sweaty bodies looked so much better than the paleness I saw back home. Eating habits seemed to fall more naturally toward health consciousness, and the ocean air was invigorating. My spirit shone as brightly as the sun sparkled on the water. And, I met a man at the gym.

After I returned to Indiana with Autumn, I competed in the Mid-States Classic and won second place. The woman who won went onto competitions that allowed steroid use which I refused to do. I wanted to stay drug-free and feminine rather than doped up and artificially big. To me, the second place win was a huge success.

I also tried to get to know the man I'd met in the gym because it had been a while since I'd had a relationship. For months, we talked and just as I thought it could go somewhere, I was out $800 and a couch. Upon investigation, I'd been duped by the lies of an alcoholic. Not wanting to wallow, I decided it was time to move on.

The California trip had been great, and I'd briefly entertained the thought of moving there for a relationship. Moving now didn't seem like too much of a stretch. California had a fresher take on nutrition. California was sunnier. California was new and exciting, whereas Indiana was the same old and people looked at me funny when I brought up vegetarianism. Suddenly, I had more to gain going towards the unknown than I did staying with what I knew.

In a matter of two weeks, my daughter and I were going to California to start a new life. I had quit my job, traded my car in for an older pickup truck, packed the things we couldn't live without into a U-Haul trailer and sold the rest. My mother agreed to fly Autumn to California where she lived with her husband, so I didn't have to travel with a small child. My father gave me a gas card and was willing to pay for a return ticket for a friend. This way, I wouldn't have to make the drive alone. With $2000 to my name and a full U-Haul, I was ready to go.

Saying goodbye to my father was the hardest. His affair with another woman had begun when I was in high school and had slowly taken him away from our close family unit. The charade had been hard for me to see and even harder for me to accept. I still remembered him as the lifeguard of our family, but he was becoming a strange new person because of her.

Through tears and too many emotional bear hugs, he tucked me into my new truck, and I drove out of Kokomo to pick up my friend, Kat, in St. Louis. We had our fun and our challenges but made it to California in three days. The scenery of America flew by as we laughed until the tears blurred our vision, and we had to straighten up again. We spent one night in a grungy hotel where we were sure the manager was going to murder us. Moving the dresser in front of the door didn't help us sleep any better. We jack-knifed the trailer in front of a diner, in the desert, that seemed to be out of the Twilight Zone. Covering the miles quickly, we went from scared to death, to overwhelmed by the beauty, but the day we overdosed on chocolate laxatives, we only wanted a toilet! It was April 1990, and we arrived just before Easter.

As my daughter and I began our new life, everything just fell into place. In Cardiff by the Sea, I found an efficiency apartment attached to a family's home who was very welcoming and even willing to care for Autumn occasionally. It was uphill from a gorgeous seaside market and a Gold's Gym where I immediately landed a job as a personal fitness trainer. Autumn fit right into the little elementary school and amassed some lifelong friends.

We would ride my bike to Miracles Café to get a bagel and hot cocoa for Autumn and a blueberry bran muffin and latte for me before going to school or the gym in the mornings. We hung out all weekend on the beach, and she could play with the neighborhood kids in the alley until I was through training clients during the week. We were home. We were a team, and we were happy.

Dedication

My new job at Gold's Gym allowed me to build my clientele, on the side, and I was quickly able to find new clients. My body was my resume, and it was outstanding. Two years earlier, when I'd begun working out in the gym in Indiana, it was simply as a stress reliever. I'd had a job working with special needs kids, within the public school system, and it was not only hard work with the children but also difficult to deal with the business side of disability. It could be extremely rewarding, and I loved it, but I needed an outlet.

After I'd been encouraged to enter into the bodybuilding competition, I'd begun to work with Mr. Indiana. He had upped my workouts and taught me that diet plays a huge part in sculpting the body you want. Soon, I was lifting weights every day for at least an hour plus an additional 20 minutes of heart-pounding cardio three times a week. I loved the endurance part of training, but it was the diet part that required intense dedication.

I ate every three hours. In the morning, I had egg whites or oatmeal made with water. Most other meals consisted of three ounces of skinless chicken breast or a small can of water-packed tuna, a half cup of green vegetables and either a half cup of rice or half of a baked potato or yam. Everything was plain. No butter, no sugar, no fruit, no alcohol, and the only carbohydrates came from the rice or potato. I had stopped eating beef and pork when I was 19 for ethical reasons.

Within two weeks of this regimen, my body transformed. The fat melted off, and my body became more defined, almost chiseled. I felt awesome and looked incredible. I found the control I had over my own body to be intoxicating. Three months later, I'd place third in my first bodybuilding competition. The bodybuilding bug had officially struck, and I have been hooked on gym life ever since.

The private clients outside of Gold's Gym piled up, and I was making $25-$30 an hour just to start. I also continued to train hard. Some of the best athletes came into Gold's, and I didn't let the opportunity pass. I'd been working and training for about four months when an old, bald man with broken glasses and bunions poking out of the holes in his shoes tapped me on the back.

Without any introduction, he said, "Honey, give me two years of your life, and I will make you unstoppable."

I said, "Okay."

The man's name was Maylen, and he'd been the strength training coach for the Oakland Raiders for 19 years. He had also trained with some of the best, most well-known bodybuilders of Venice Beach. Now, for no reason apparent to me, his main focus and goal in life seemed to be training me and stopping at nothing less than the top.

Whenever I had an extra hour, he was there. He barked at me, "Watch the clock," allowing me no more than 30 seconds of rest in between sets of his grueling workout schedule. He challenged me to go beyond the point of pain and do at least two more repetitions. He was creating a champion, and I thrived on the whole process. The attention, the training, and the outcome pushed me harder. Soon my 5'4", 115-pound frame was bench pressing 150 pounds, squatting 250 pounds and doing over 12 pull-ups in a row.

At this same time, I was also working with a new client who was very heavy into a supplement company called Omnitrition. Developed by well-known scientists, Durk Pearson and Sandy Shaw, there were fiber and protein powders as well as products for fat loss, lean muscle gain, energy and mental clarity. My client noticed the dedication I had and asked if I'd like to try some. I began taking many of them and immediately felt a difference.

There was a huge Southern California bodybuilding competition in Palm Springs the next year that I wanted to compete in, and I already knew I was going in better prepared than for any competition I'd been in previously in Indiana. My ammunition was threefold: Coach Maylen, Omnitrition and my new life of progress in California.

My Perfect Storm

As our first summer in California continued, Autumn and I lived in bliss. She'd finished kindergarten, and many of her friends were headed into the first grade with her. I was enjoying all the work I had between Gold's, my private clients, and my personal training. We went to the beach often, and I got Autumn a kitten and a pet rat. She sang songs and pretended to be Ariel from *The Little Mermaid*. A new client was a vocal coach. I traded voice lessons for training which was both adorable and confidence boosting for Autumn. Though I remained driven in both work and bodybuilding, she was always my first priority.

I had been 23 when her father and I had gotten pregnant during a spring break trip to Florida. I was going to Purdue, and he went to Ball State about two hours away, but spring break doesn't care. My dad had tried to play rational and urged me to get an abortion, but I was adamant about keeping the baby. Even though I wasn't in a steady relationship, I knew I was not going to let this baby go. I already loved her, and I didn't even know anything about her yet.

Having always been active in my life, I wasn't going to let pregnancy slow me down. I rode my bike to classes, continued to springboard dive and even went water skiing up at our lake house in Culver, Indiana. At the 28 week mark, I remember going to the Purdue-Notre Dame football game and the Greek Fest while experiencing the rock hard belly of Braxton-Hicks contractions. The next morning, after finding blood in my panties, I went to the doctor to find I was already beginning to dilate. I was immediately put on bed rest. After a week, I had dilated another half centimeter and was admitted to the hospital for more bed rest and an IV.

My baby girl became my companion. I would talk to her and put headphones on my belly so she could listen better. When the nurses wouldn't let me get up to pee or take a shower, I told myself to deal with it. They washed me and took me on wheelchair trips to sit in front of the premature infant ward. The babies were so tiny and hooked up to lots of tubes and monitors.

For nine days, nurses took down all the vitals of both my baby and me. There were steroid shots to speed up the development of Autumn's lungs that were quite painful. The lack of activity was opposite everything I had stood for in my life, but I was going to do everything in my power to keep creating the life I carried inside.

At thirty weeks, I was sent home with pills and told to 'hold on' for at least another two weeks. At this point, Autumn was fully positioned for birth. My pelvis felt like it was split in half, and I felt pressure constantly. Two weeks later, the perfect storm arrived, and I got to the hospital four centimeters dilated.

Twelve hours of extreme pressure, cramping, back labor, and uncontrollable farting later, I broke the leather straps of the hospital bed and gave birth to a beautiful, angelic baby girl. It was far from the quiet, music-filled, peaceful birth I had dreamed of, but, I withstood the worst odds and had done it. Small, perfect, and precious, Autumn Dawn took her first breaths, unassisted, before she was whisked away to an incubator.

After two days, I was sent home alone, sad and sore but full of the idea that I had a gorgeous baby girl. All the work of overriding emotion to give life to another human being, the discomfort of giving myself up so another could be born, was quickly forgotten as I laid a gentle touch on her. Her smell, her small four-pound body without fully formed toenails, gave purpose to the pain, worry, and struggle. Being so tiny and premature, she couldn't co-ordinate sucking and breathing, so I pumped breast milk to give to her through tubes. For three weeks, she lived in the incubator. I was allowed to be with her for 15 minutes every three hours. I never missed an opportunity.

By the time my baby came home, she was able to breastfeed, and she was up to four- pounds, fourteen ounces. She looked like a doll in the car seat. For a month, she slept in a pulled out dresser drawer right next to me in the bed, so I could make sure she was breathing throughout the night. This child of mine was my pride and joy. My life changed forever the second I found out about her. Though it hasn't been without tears and challenges, my life has been better with her in it.

A Star Is Born

The California summer settled into fall, and Autumn and I kept a furious pace. We wanted to take advantage of everything we could. In September, an audition opened up at a local theater for *The Sound of Music*. Back in Indianapolis, we'd gone to a production together when Autumn was four. She'd looked me straight in the eye and told me that one day she was going to play Gretel. This was her chance.

At the auditions, the lines of little girls and moms were outrageous. Once each girl made it up to the judges, she was asked a few questions and then asked to sing a song. Since Autumn had been working with my vocal coach client, she had no fear when it came to her turn. Within a couple of days, I got a callback, and the rehearsals started.

Rehearsals were grueling. Almost every night for two or three hours, we went to practice for the next 12 weeks. During this time, I was also training for the Palm Springs Desert Classic bodybuilding competition. Between the show rehearsals, the extra time I put in to help the production, as a stage mom, and my hard training schedule for both myself and my clients, our time was stretched and brutally scheduled.

Opening night of *The Sound of Music* finally arrived. Family members from all over the country had come to see Autumn, and we were all there, front and center. The curtain went up, and the opening scenes rolled by beautifully until all of the Von Trapp children were whistled to march in. All of them filed on stage, except one. Technically, a Gretel was in attendance, but it was not Autumn.

Quicker than lightning, I was running backstage. I found Autumn laying in the lap of another stage mom, rubbing her stomach. She had thrown up, presumably from the week's hub-bub of family coming into town and the pressure of dress rehearsals, but typical Autumn, she was bent on trying again. In every scene after that, she was perfect and soon declared that her new favorite thing was performing in front of a full house. The success of *The Sound of Music* followed Autumn for years. She continued to be a star in many more productions.

As Autumn was flexing her stage chops, I continued training as hard as I could with Coach Maylen and taking the Omnitrition products. Just like in the beginning when I had started training with Mr. Indiana, I watched in amazement as my body changed. Muscle mass and strength increased exponentially, yet I stayed lean.

At one point, I'd gained more than ten pounds, reaching 125 pounds. Maylen said that I looked awesome and asked me to consider powerlifting since I was so strong for my size. He also told me to eat more, even going as far as to suggest getting up in the middle of the night to eat an egg or a spoonful of peanut butter. I did not like what I saw though, so I cut back on the amount of food I was eating until I got back to a comfortable 114 pounds.

At this point, my diet was very similar to the diet leading up to the Mid-States Classic in Indiana. Most of my protein came from egg whites, water-packed tuna (or sashimi now that I lived in an area with fresh access) or skinless chicken breasts. I stayed away from sugar, fruit, dairy, alcohol, salt, fat and strictly limited the number of starchy carbohydrates I ate. This was a "carb deplete" cycle of the typical bodybuilding yo-yo diet. As competition time neared, I moved into the "carb load" part of the diet when I ate yams, rice or rice cakes every few hours. The overload of carbohydrates acted as a filler for my new lean muscles and plumped them up, accentuating every bump and curve.

When the Palm Springs Desert Classic competition arrived, it was Easter Sunday. Autumn woke up in our hotel room with my mom and a huge Easter basket. I ate a hard-boiled egg and got an application of skin dye, which is makeup for muscles. Then, I took my place among the hundreds of other girls in line for orientation. There were so many in my weight class. I started to make some mental comparisons but was careful not to overthink it all and get intimidated.

Before the judging began, and we were all getting ready, I was approached by one of the judges. Though our conversation started friendly enough, it quickly turned into an offer extended from the head judge to sway the competition in my favor if I would extend him a special courtesy. This judge left little to the imagination as he explained how the head judge really liked blondes. Disgusted at the audacity of both judges, I coldly answered that I was not available and brushed past him. I blocked the encounter from my mind, so I could focus on the monumental task that lay ahead of me.

At the weigh-in, I qualified for the 112 pound lightweight class limit since I was 111 pounds with a svelte 9% body fat. On average, women have 20% body fat with athletes having between 12-18%. I was quite chiseled at 9%. Most of the morning judging consisted of showing the mandatory poses where each contestant flexed a specific muscle group while holding everything else tight. The judges asked each of us to come up and showcase certain parts. Then, they arranged us accordingly, in rows, with the favorites positioned closest to them. They called some up more than others, and sometimes, they wanted us to hold the poses for what seemed like an eternity. It was part endurance test and part beauty pageant.

There was a break between the morning and evening judging. I used the time to eat and to prepare for the upcoming 90-second dance routine each of us had to do. Knowing that the majority of the judging was done and the competition's end was near, I relaxed a bit. The feeling was mutual because once the dance routines began, the entertainment value of the show shot up. With music, spotlights and ESPN cameras everywhere, I went out on stage and danced my heart out to Neil Diamond's "Coming to America." I finished off with a standing backflip, breathless but full of pride.

For the rest of the competition, I sat in the audience with Autumn and my mom and downed a bag of peanut M&M's. It was a long-awaited treat that was relished as I shared it with my daughter. When the results came in, I stood second tallest on the podium, losing to the training partner of the head judge. After having the slimy conversation with the other judge, I could only imagine what went on during those training sessions. Not to be discouraged, the second place win brought my name into the fray of bodybuilders to watch. I also found out that I received the most airtime on the ESPN cameras. We went out for pizza in celebration.

For days after the pizza and candy celebration, my digestive tract went haywire. I had not eaten any fats, sweets or heavy grease-soaked carbs in so long; my gallbladder could not handle the bombardment. My body shut down, and I lost a lot of weight, but I had just won second place in my first big California competition. I was stoked. My name was getting recognition and Omnitrition wanted to sponsor me in all of my future events. I became their new poster girl.

Up until this point, all of the competitions I had entered were sanctioned by the National Physique Committee. The NPC circuit had no drug regulations and, though I saw a clear disadvantage to not using growth-enhancing drugs, I did not use drugs nor did I want to compete with girls who did. I was also bothered by the blatant sexual politics within the organization. I chose to compete less than six months later in the American Natural Bodybuilding Conference's California Championships. Girls from nearby states would be there, and we would all be drug-free.

When Autumn heard that I was going to be competing again in such a short time, she told me she was going to go live with her grandmother because I got too grouchy. Even at such a young age, she saw how the bodybuilding diets made me irritable. She would yell at me to eat something when my blood sugar dropped dangerously low. At the same time, she was also rehearsing for another play, so our quality time together was getting thin.

Before either of us knew it, the lights of competition time were upon us again. This time, I weighed in at 108 pounds and 7% body fat. I loved it. I felt great, and I looked great. I was getting impressive recognition and feedback for the physique I had created. My thinking was the leaner, the better. My menstrual cycles had stopped way back when I cut out all the fat from my diet, but what woman wouldn't love that?

I came out in my teeny, tiny bikini and modeled each pose when asked. Every position highlighted specific muscle areas, but I had to keep the rest of my body tight. So, the ten or fifteen seconds felt like hours. Again, the judges called contestants randomly and placed them according to what they saw. After the mandatory poses, I performed a shortened version of my 90-second dance routine without any music. It was demanding and stressful since most of the judging occurred during these morning hours.

During the evening show, all of us performed the full 90-second dance routine with music. More relaxed than that morning, I whipped through my routine. I had carved my body over the last few years, and this was the time to show it off. My muscles glistened with sweat. My naturally, white, blonde hair accentuated everything that was 'California.' This was all the high that I needed in my life.

I was amazed when they called my name and presented me with the biggest trophy. It even lit up. That moment will stand out in time forever. I was surprised and honored and knew that I hadn't done it alone. I motioned for my young daughter to hop up on stage with me. She flew into my arms, and with mile-wide smiles on our faces, we shot bicep poses to the cameras.

Just like that, I had a center page story in the Female Bodybuilding magazine, and agents and anyone who worked out in Southern California knew my name. This was the recognition I wanted for creating and sculpting my body. Little did I know my drive for the leaner body would nearly kill me, but it would also create a life of passion and purpose.

Hello Violence

Post competition, my name was passed around like a celebrity's. Agents and photographers lined up for my name and number. Everyone wanted a piece of me provided I sign a waiver letting them do anything they wanted with my image and brand. A new athletic club hit Southern California, and I was asked to be a part of it. Coach Maylen came, too. My clientele quickly grew at whatever rates I set, and Omnitrition had projects lined up for miles.

Autumn and I moved from our small efficiency apartment, next to the garage, to a townhome with a gorgeous total ocean view. We shared this great space with the head aerobics instructor at the new athletics club. Sadly, after about six months, she decided to move in with her boyfriend, and we could no longer afford the rent on our own. I had been casually seeing a man for about a month, and he offered to let us stay at his house until we found a place.

Thank goodness it was only two months. This guy ended up rearing a scorpion tail of control and jealousy issues, along with house rules that made it difficult ever to relax. He was generous with his money and bought many lovely gifts for both Autumn and me, but there were always conditions for me. If I wanted to wear short skirts or shorts anywhere but his house, he'd say, "Those are my legs" and not let me out of the house unless he went with me.

Unfortunately, this was not my first controlling and abusive boyfriend. When I was a junior in high school, I'd been dating a senior who planned to move away for college. Not wanting to be without a boyfriend my last year of high school, I'd broken up with him. Immediately, I'd started dating another football star, and everything had gone back to wonderful until the abuse began.

The first incident was minor. He got angry and pushed me down. I only hurt my knee a little. He apologized so profusely it surprised me. He had gone so far as to say he wanted to break up, so he wouldn't hurt me again. I could tell he was sorry, so I said no. I honestly believed it wouldn't happen again.

Over time, one hard push grew into throwing, punching, and face slapping. He locked me in the bedroom once, saying I could not come out until he let me out. I caught him sitting naked on the couch with a likewise naked woman. He said they were just watching TV and nothing happened. At a Boston concert, he slammed me against a wall and nearly broke my rib. It was painful, and I wanted to call my dad, but the apologies came again.

He claimed he never remembered these actions after his rage subsided. Occasionally, he would come out of his anger to go into a catatonic-like state and sit there numbly or rock himself silently in a corner. Other times, he'd grab scissors or other items close by that could inflict damage and threaten suicide if I ever tried to leave.

I fell for all of it. I knew I'd feel guilty if something happened to him because I did or did not do something his way. I stayed in the sick, abusive game and somehow believed I deserved it. I felt that I was showing him the only love he'd ever had in his life, trusting that he would change, thinking that it could stop.

For a year after graduating from high school, I continued to live at home and work as I attended community college and dated this boyfriend. We decided to move in together, and I moved into the abusive relationship even deeper. When his anger would rise, I would remain calm which, in turn, made his anger boil even higher. He'd get a killer look in his eyes, and the veins on his forehead would throb explosively. Immediately after, he would lash out. Once, he threw me across a coffee table.

When he admitted he had an anger problem and asked me to find him help, I pounced on the chance. I made the appointment only to find out later that he had stormed out of the office. The doctor called me and warned me that my boyfriend was a pathological liar and could be very dangerous. It would be better if I stayed away from him.

Contrary to the doctor's warning, I continued to live with this boyfriend because I knew he had a good heart. I was determined to help and to change him. I thought, through love and acceptance, anything was possible. This was my motto when I taught autistic children; however, in this case, it did not work. Despite my best intentions, there were more drunken late night arrivals, more violent episodes and one night he thought he was Jesus. He'd come home drunk and high, and if he wanted sex, he'd take it whether or not I felt the same.

I was 19, working the night shift full-time at a hospital, attending school during the day, majoring in psychology, and suddenly, I was pregnant. He told me to get rid of the "goddamn baby" and tried to push me down the stairs. Luckily, I caught the railing and saved myself from falling all the way down. After even more threats, I finally packed his bags and left them by the door.

I wanted to keep the baby. My parents were concerned that with my age, my schooling unfinished and the fact that I would forever be attached to this abusive man, I should get an abortion. My grandfather whom I loved so much went through great pains to show me support no matter what decision I made. I went to counseling. I was worried I would be killing a spirit, a soul. The minister said no. Whether he was correct or not, an abortion was scheduled in Indianapolis.

The night before I was going to the appointment with my parents, I was alone in my apartment. I couldn't sleep. To numb my mind, I turned on the TV. The Discovery Channel was showing a documentary on the development of a fetus in utero. They showed a ten week old with feet, hands, finger, and toes. My baby was just turning ten weeks. Devastated, I laid on the floor and cried all night.

The procedure was barbaric at best. I was on the table with my legs strapped open when the doctor who was examining me calls for another young male doctor to "come look at this cervix." I was barely twenty, embarrassed and terrified beyond words. A nurse walked up to hold my hand. She told me to squeeze as hard as I wanted and not to hold my breath. A very loud sucker vacuum machine turned on.

By the time he stopped the machine, I was sobbing and pleading for him to please be done. He said he had to make sure he got all the parts out so infection wouldn't set in. "All of the body parts," he said. Emotional and hurt, I was wheeled off into recovery. In the next bed, was a large black woman who had four kids at home and couldn't afford another. We both lay there, with hitching sobs and in gut-wrenching pain.

After two hours of recovery, the bleeding subsided. I remember being wheeled out in a wheelchair and sitting mute in the back seat on the way home. My parents stopped to eat, but I wasn't hungry. As we pulled into the driveway of our family home, my ex-boyfriend pulled up behind us. He said he wanted to drive me back to the apartment and take care of me.

Too tired to fight and thinking that he may also be distraught, I went with him. He'd barely helped me into the apartment before he'd begun calling me a murderer. Those horrible moments, in the apartment that night, have always added to the weight of one day every year. My expected due date had been February 14th, Valentine's Day, 1980.

Letting Go

For several years, in Cardiff by the Sea, it was just the Dawn and Autumn Show. After the big bodybuilding win, I was kept busy with travel, more competitions, infomercials, and even a BBC film. Autumn continued to be amazing in school as well as on the stage. She was blossoming into a little star, and I was climbing up my ladder of fame.

Autumn performed in at least two musical productions every year, and she joined another theatrical company, so she was busy nearly every day. She also signed on with two talent agencies and took private acting lessons. Between rehearsals, lessons and auditions, we were driving all over San Diego and many times back and forth to Los Angeles, too. Over five years, she did multiple commercials, one infomercial, and several print jobs. Money was always offered, but it wasn't ever much, and I never thought to negotiate. The experiences that Autumn was receiving were lifelong lessons, so the money was a secondary bonus that I didn't question.

Omnitrition took me all over the world. I was treated like a queen in speaking and guest posing in front of thousands. They sponsored me, all expenses paid, to the East Coast Nationals for two years in a row. In addition to my work with Omnitrition, I also did two infomercials for a home gym company, made an exercise video, and a BBC short film. I was paid for doing the video, given a home gym for the infomercial, and got my pick of all the supplements I wanted for the BBC film. Again, I graciously took what was offered. I was too caught up in the feeling of stardom to ask for more. Perhaps, I was naïve. Maybe, I was just too amazed to realize there could be more than what Autumn and I were already getting. I felt we had a good thing going.

During the summer of 1992, Autumn was scheduled to spend nine weeks at the Culver Military Academy back in Indiana. This was a prestigious school of year-round programs like aeronautics, equestrian training, and sailing that were taught in a rigid military style. The winter program took high school-aged kids only, and the summer program took children as early as age nine.

When Autumn and I still lived in Indiana, my family had a lake house on the same lake that bordered the military academy. We had spent many times relaxing at the house, watching the cadets march through the campus or the crew team row in the lake. Autumn had always told her great-grandfather that she wanted to go there.

He had attended for many years as did my father, uncles, and I. My father and grandfather were in the Black Horse Troop which appears in the Presidential Inaugural Parades. At age thirteen, I'd taken inspiration from my father who had learned to trick ride there and attended a special summer program for English horseback riding. It was an intense two-week program with training in horse riding and caretaking as well as performing in shows at the end of each week.

So when Autumn was finally old enough to go, my grandfather, her great-grandfather, willingly paid for the whole thing as well as both of our plane tickets, so I could help her get settled in. We were just weeks away from leaving when my mother called me. She asked to meet for coffee. I was sitting in the parking lot beside Starbucks in Del Mar when an eerie sensation crept through me. I looked over to see my mom walking toward me, and I started screaming. Before she was able to tell me, I knew my grandfather had passed away.

He had been sitting up in bed with a book in his lap and his reading glasses still on. A great white owl was seen outside his window, and a feather was dropped the evening before he died. This meant the passing of a great one.

My grandfather was great, indeed. He had been a prominent figure in Kokomo. As the owner and publisher of the *Kokomo Tribune*, he'd made it the top-selling newspaper per capita in the country. He'd also had partial ownership in Kokomo Opalescent Glass and seemed to own half the town, via real estate or business management, throughout the years. Captain of the Yacht Club at Ocean Reef in Key Largo, Florida, Grandpa Blacklidge was also president of many committees, contributed to the higher education for the underprivileged, and donated to numerous charities. In spite of all his achievements, love and care for the family was always his first and most passionate priority. His vigilant protection and influence in our family was paramount and felt, as I'd moved through life.

When I had been in my first abusive relationship and headed to a forced abortion, he had written me a heartfelt letter. In it, he'd lamented on how rough life is and how it presented us with many difficult decisions to make and challenges to overcome. He was sad that I was embroiled in such a complicated one, at such a young age, and reminded me how much I was loved no matter what the outcome. It meant the world to me.

Since he was always there in my childhood, his presence meant safety for me. He was a pillar of strength in our family, and I loved him so much. He had come out to California when Autumn was starring in *The Sound of Music,* and that was the last time we'd seen him. When Autumn got into Culver Military Academy, we were supposed to spend time together as we got her settled. Instead, we spent the time saying goodbye at his funeral. It was a very bitter-sweet moment to be able to see Autumn following in our family's footsteps yet not have Grandpa Blacklidge there to see it.

The span of time that Autumn was at Culver Military Academy was the longest she and I had spent apart. Because the rules of the Academy were so strict, she was allowed no visitors or phone calls for the first two weeks. For the remaining seven weeks, my father was her weekend visitor and was there for any outings that allowed visitors. I flew back to surprise her, at the end of camp, and watch her in the closing ceremonies. For her big finale, she fired the rocket that she had made during the program. Everyone watched the straight line of smoke go high into the air. Elated that her rocket worked perfectly and excited to see me, she came running into my arms. I was enormously proud of her and relieved to be reunited with her.

Full Plate

*A*utumn and I had become a team. From early on, it had been just the two of us. Her father and I hadn't found enough common ground to stay together. We divorced after a year. Since I'd only had three months of schooling left until graduation when I'd gotten pregnant with Autumn, I wanted to finish so that I could have my degree. Autumn and I had moved into my dad's basement, and then on our own, in a small one bedroom apartment, in student housing. I had enrolled full-time at Purdue University and applied for food stamps and WIC benefits (Women, Infants, and Children). If I couldn't find an affordable babysitter, I brought Autumn to class and sat in the back. If she fussed, I quietly gave her a bottle.

Amazingly, it had worked out well enough that I graduated just four months after returning. Remember, I had had to drop out only three months shy of graduating when my pregnancy with Autumn had reached high risk. Completing my remaining credits as a single mother and graduating with honors with a Bachelor of Science in Child Development and Family Sciences, with a minor in Psychology, made me feel like Super Woman. The next month,

I had re-enrolled with the idea that I would gain another degree in Neonatal Nursing because of my experience birthing and caring for premature Autumn in the NICU (Neonatal Intensive Care Unit).

I quickly found out I am not Super Woman and dropped out of school. I needed a break, but more importantly, I needed a job and money. When I found a good directorship at the Northern Indiana State Hospital (NISH) in South Bend, Indiana, I bought a little mobile home in a clean park just across the state line in Niles, Michigan. Our neighbors were nice, and one of the women ran a small daycare that had a spot open that Autumn could take. When I left in the morning, Autumn would scream and cry until she puked. After being by my side nearly all of the time, she was not accepting my regular nine to five job.

For weeks, this behavior continued. I felt horrendously guilty. When she finally stopped, I began trying to get her to sleep in her own bed. At two years old, she only wanted to sleep right next to me. Ignoring her screams for mommy broke my heart. Again, she'd cry until she gagged and vomited. She learned how to climb out of her crib and would try to make it down the hall to my room. Many mornings, I would find her asleep in the hallway. She'd had enough energy to make it out of her crib but not enough to make it all the way to my bedroom.

My boss, Dr. Tim, offered to come over one evening and sat with me while Autumn screamed to get out of her crib to sleep with me. He said she needed to learn to comfort herself and fall asleep without the need to be with me. It felt wrong for me to let her get so upset, but, he, being a Ph.D. in Child Psychology, insisted this is what she needed. Ultimately, what he needed was to try to get in my pants while she was in bed. I resisted, and he hesitantly stopped and agreed that a boss/employee relationship should remain platonic.

NISH had many employees that did not like the fact that a young white girl, just out of college, had seniority over them. The direct care staff did soften up, after a bit, when they saw I was no threat and only there to ensure the best programming for the thirty-two special needs children in the unit. A cook named Maury ended up being my nightmare at NISH.

Maury was a soft-spoken black cook that would visit my office whenever he would deliver food to the unit. He was kind at first, but when he asked me on a date, and I turned him down, the violence erupted. He slammed me against the water fountain screaming it was because of his skin color. I explained as I shook with fear that it had nothing to do with that, but I knew he was married. I did not date married men. A few days later, my wallet was stolen from my office, and $2,000 of charges came up on my card that he had made. He also threatened my life and that of my baby daughter, so the police were called. I sent Autumn to live with my mother for a few weeks. I tied my doors shut on my trailer home and slept with a knife. I had never felt so scared for my life. He was ultimately caught and put in prison.

Just after Autumn turned two years old, I noticed her putting her ear up to the TV and not coming when I called her. At first, I dismissed the behavior as usual toddler sassiness. Then, I realized that all the bouts of croup, bronchitis, and ear infections that she had resulting from her weakened and premature immune system may have damaged something. I took her to an ear, nose, and throat specialist who confirmed 80% hearing loss in one ear and 20% in the other due to built-up scar tissue. In addition to her ears, Autumn's tonsils and adenoids were also swollen and constricted her air capacity. The doctor ordered an allergy test. The surgery was done and the blood work revealed dairy and wheat allergies.

By this time in my life, I was already eating fairly cleanly. My mother had cut out refined sugars and processed foods, started gardening and canning the harvests, and instilling a healthy lifestyle all while I was still a teenager. Soon after the abortion, I had read a book on corporate farming and the cruelty within the industry and quit eating red meat. I still occasionally ate fish and chicken but made sure that both were harvested sustainably. Finding out I needed to cut out dairy and wheat from my daughter's diet, in the mid-1980's, was a feat. We drank rice milk and bought rice or almond cheese, but the wheat thing was challenging, so I was not so obsessed with that. By eliminating dairy from our diet, both of us experienced improved health. Autumn could breathe with ease, and the number of infections drastically was reduced. As I found new products and tips, we were soon eating no red meat and no dairy and strictly limiting the wheat, all in the name of better overall health.

After a year at NISH, I realized that I was deeply invested in the development of the children in my unit yet missing out on some of the most impressionable days of Autumn's developing life. Though we went adventuring almost every weekend, the five day work week plus the commute time was taking away valuable quality time. I decided to quit my job and return to school at Purdue. The move brought us closer to my family. I was offered a part-time graduate staff position, and Autumn was accepted into the Purdue Child Development Lab School. With my schooling, I was able to observe her as well as teach the children in other age groups.

A year and a half flew by, and I was twelve credits away from completing my Masters. It was getting tough financially, and if Autumn was not in the Lab School, she was often with a sitter. When I had her with me, I was studying. Finally, she got to a point where enough was enough. The night she climbed onto my lap, threw my books on the floor, and said, "No more study, Mommy, play with me," a chord was struck. I could always come back and finish a degree, but these days with Autumn only come by once. I had one chance to be a good mother.

We moved back to Indianapolis and into a funky little house in the Broadripple area with my sister. I took a job teaching at the Indianapolis Child Development Center, and Autumn got into the preschool in the same building. We were back together again. For eight months, we lived amongst the free-spirited hippies, food co-ops, organic vegetarian restaurants and music venues of Broadripple. After that, my sister moved closer to her boyfriend, whom she would later marry, and I decided it was time to go home to Kokomo. That was when I took the job with autistic children. The job caused so much stress that I started working out in the gym.

My year teaching autistic children was both rewarding and very draining. I had a motto on a banner across my classroom saying, "teach through love and acceptance." I was going to approach these boys, ages five through eighteen, in an entirely new manner. The padded "time out room" was now a room of acceptance. Every day I would take each child in there for a time and just sit with them and do what they did: no expectations, no talking, or toys…just being One with them. Amazing things happened, particularly with my youngest most severe child. Henry was five. He was not potty trained, did not speak, spun everything, and would pull his hair or scratch with frustration. He was like an animal child when he first arrived in my care. But after weeks of our ritual, he began to 'come out.' First, he would look me in the eye. Then, he would sit in my lap and take my hand and rub it gently up and down his arm. He started hugging me and trying to communicate. I felt our souls were connecting.

After the school year, I offered to take Henry every day for two weeks to give his mother a break. My 4-year-old daughter and I began to teach him sign language and take him swimming. He loved the water. After pool time, he would sign "cookie," and I would treat him. We also took him out to eat to teach social skills. I loved that little boy and always wondered what happened to him when I decided to not return to the classroom the following fall.

Sick Obsession

For the next couple of years in California, our lives continued to be hectic yet awesome. We moved quite a bit but always stayed in the Del Mar/ Cardiff by the Sea area. I continued to train both myself and many clients. Autumn continued to amaze at school. From frugal living and avid savings, I finally decided that it was time to own a home.

After a lot of looking, we found a fixer-upper condo on the LaCosta Golf Course that was darling. It was in foreclosure and owned by the bank, so it was a great deal. When we first looked at it, all I could think was how bad it stunk because it had been shut up for so long. The realtor said that there had been a little flood, so the carpet was wet, stained, and very stinky, but it had gorgeous Mexican pink tile in the entryway and kitchen, two bedrooms, two bathrooms and was just steps from the swimming pool. I felt it had great potential, and the price was right. After the sale, Autumn and a friend painted her room. My friend Kat and I painted a big purple sunflower in the living room and an eyeball around the peephole. It was perfect for the two of us.

During the three years that we lived in this condo, I became even more focused on my diet. I got swept up in the vegetarian and then vegan crazes that were taking the nation. Besides, I threw my extreme twist in by sticking to the bodybuilder's pre-contest diet year-round. Typically, bodybuilders ease up on their diet in the offseason to rebuild and sustain their bodies and are quite successful with yo-yo diets. I loved the lean, symmetrical tanned look that the competition diet gave me. With my long, naturally, white blond hair, I was known as the ultra-fit, extreme athlete. It was a title that bolstered my confidence because I alone had all of the control.

All of my other competitors were gaining muscle size as I was just getting leaner. The judges at the Nationals two years in a row commented on it, too. The first year, I placed second in the nation and the following year, third. I felt awesome. Around this time, I fired my beloved Coach Maylen. He was treating me more and more like a Raiders football player. This was only amplified as his drinking also increased. We both loved each other as a coach and trainer and knew that neither of us would have achieved what we had without the other. I just couldn't handle his alcohol abuse and neither could the gym. He was fired from there as well.

The diets in the early 21st century leaned toward high carbohydrates and low fats which lead to an increase in obesity and diabetes. I began to research veganism and raw food, the macrobiotic diet, Mr. Macdougall's diet, and the Atkin's diet. The Macdougall diet and the Atkins diets are almost opposite. Macdougall's is plant and carbohydrate-based with no added fats whereas the

Atkin's diet leans toward high fat and animal proteins with little carbohydrates.

As a result of my narrow-mindedness of what I would or would not eat, I started to eat fewer macronutrients I needed to train the way I did but also to live. I got sick more and went to the doctor's more often, thinking I was sick due to some autoimmune disease. Odd rashes were appearing, as were blood blisters in my mouth, and my fingers were blue a lot because my circulation was so poor. I went to a rheumatologist who sent me to an oncologist. I had plenty of blood tests, a bone marrow biopsy, and an upper endoscopy. All the results confirmed I had severe anemia and was celiac (allergic to wheat) like Autumn. My extreme focus on my diet planning told me that I couldn't eat any grains at all. The list of no's growing longer: no sugar, no fruit because of the sugar content, no dairy, no alcohol, no salt, no fat and now, no grains, including wheat.

Feeling like I was at the top of my game and now, that Autumn was in freshman high school, I started dating again. I hadn't dated much after Autumn's father. I'd always felt that my daughter was my first priority and my training my second, so our schedules were constantly pressed for time. There had only been three relationships, and they all were short-lived as well as fallen short of any expectations I'd had of love. After we'd moved out of Broadripple and went back home to Kokomo, I had started dating a guy I'd previously known but never dated. He was great for a couple of months but then started being controlling and jealous. After that was the liar whom I'd met in California and was in part, responsible for me moving to California. Lastly, there was the guy

I moved in with after I won first place, and the new Club opened. He also turned out to be hideously jealous.

Finally comfortable in my job, my life and my skin, I felt good when I noticed a very handsome and fit man watching me at the Club. I started watching him, too. He was a triathlete and took the spinning classes two or three times a week. I finally took charge and introduced myself. We went out a couple of times, outside of the Club, and he offered to buy me all I needed to start spinning. He bought it all—shorts, shoes, a cycling shirt and the cool socks. I took classes with him and immediately got addicted to the cardio high.

Our relationship grew over the next six months. This man was pure class, and it was great to have a boyfriend again. Then, I found out he was married. Supposedly, they had so much wealth tied together; it was easier for tax purposes to stay married but live as separated. I was heartbroken, but since we were getting serious, we both thought it best to break up. We talked on the phone a few times, but everything just fizzled and vanished. Through it all, I did find a new love of spinning, cycling, and cardio in general.

After that, I joined an Internet dating service. I went on quite a few dates, but none sparked any interest. Feeling adventurous, I started looking outside Southern California and almost immediately met a man in New Zealand. We started talking, and I liked what I saw. He was a native Californian but living on the North Island. He had a house on the beach, and I had always wanted to visit New Zealand. When he said that if I got my plane ticket, he'd take care of the rest, I jumped at the chance.

Without a second thought, I flew to a foreign country to meet a man I barely knew. Autumn stayed with friends and, my mother, her grandmother, was less than twenty miles away. She was very independent and self-sufficient by this time, so I was confident she would be fine. Though I knew the idea alone sounded crazy, I was not scared or worried, but I did take enough money to stay in a hotel if it was too weird.

For ten days, he was a perfect gentleman and showed me a fun and unforgettable time, but there were no sparks. I slept in his son's bunk bed, and it was apparent he was still in love with his ex-wife who lived two blocks away. It wasn't the love I'd been looking for, but the entire experience wasn't one I regret. Not many people step that far outside of their comfort zone, and I was proud to say it wasn't the first time I'd taken such a risk. Life is an adventure, and I had decided to live it with passion but also do it all my way, even if it was risky or perhaps detrimental.

Within a year, I saw an ad on another Internet dating site titled *Peaceful Warrior*. *The Way of the Peaceful Warrior* by Dan Millman is one of my all-time favorite books, so this ad caught my eye. He described himself to be a tall, Irish-Cherokee, gentle spirit who practices yoga daily and weight trains at the gym. I sent him a wink, and soon we exchanged numbers. The first time he called, I couldn't make it to the phone in time, so our machine picked up with Autumn's voice saying, "You've reached Dawn and Autumn, please leave a message." When I did answer, he asked if he had heard the message correctly because his daughter's name was Autumn, too. Things gracefully fell into place.

Our first date was a high society charity dinner to benefit the San Diego Children's Hospital. Tickets were $200 each, and he picked me up in a formal suit and tie with flowers in his hand. I was shocked for a first date. He was 6'4", tanned with beautiful brown eyes and distinguished greying, shoulder-length hair. He had driven four hours and spent a fortune for this one night with someone he didn't even know. I was quite flattered.

The next weekend, he came again from Brentwood, near Los Angeles, to Del Mar and took me walking down the beach. He noticed a colorful pinwheel spinning slowly in someone's yard and said, "Life should be like that." I fell for that deeper philosophical side, and we spent every weekend together. My attraction grew and so did a friendly relationship. He noticed my picky eating habits and would insist that I eat at least bread with my veggies. I saw that he wouldn't take no for an answer and would do as he said though I felt guilty for the carbohydrates later. It was nice to have someone care in a non-controlling manner.

After five months, he was transferred to Australia for his job, within the technology industry, and he asked me if I would come. Though I wanted to continue what we had, I refused to uproot my daughter. I told him that she was the most important thing in my life, and I did everything for her. In reality, I was not seeing how my personal blinders were affecting her. Between dieting and trying to manufacture love, my focus had gotten so linear that my happy, healthy, positive, and self-confident daughter was turning into a withdrawn, depressed teen.

Fucked Up

We loved our time in the funky condo on the LaCosta Golf Course. As always, Autumn was my shining star. She had friends, was doing quite well in school, balanced any theater or modeling parts she got with ease, and still found time for extracurricular activities. The time she spent at the Culver Military Academy handed down the Blacklidge love of horses, so we leased a horse part-time at the local stables and got her riding lessons. She began babysitting and having a social life. Our hippie neighbor taught her how to drive, and without me even knowing it, she was growing up and slipping away.

After three years, we decided to move up. The condo sold very quickly to a woman named Angela. Likely, she would enjoy our painted sunflower, eyeball peephole, and many different colored rooms. We found a four-level townhome on the other side of the golf course that was under four miles away from both Autumn's school and the gym. I gave Autumn the top floor, which had the master bedroom and bath with a big vanity, for her to get dolled up with her friends. I took the next level that also had the kitchen, an office and the dining room that overlooked the living room and fireplace below. It even had a two car garage. It was a great fit for us.

For Autumn's 16th birthday, I bought her a beautiful young chestnut thoroughbred named Layla. I also bought her a car, a Toyota Celica. She eventually burned up the engine on the Celica by not checking the oil, but the love she had for Layla only grew. She rode, groomed, and trained Layla to be an incredible jumper. After the Celica, my mom and I pitched in to get Autumn a new Ford Ranger that she could put all her gear in and drive out to the stables.

When we found out that the high school she would be attending, as a freshman, had graduating classes of over 2000 kids, we were both taken aback. Most of Autumn's schools had been smaller, and the thought of a college-sized high school turned her off. She had expressed interest in being an exchange student, so when I heard that one of my clients had a friend in England who was looking for a live-in nanny, I started looking into it. My client was from Ireland, but it was her best friend who lived in London and had two little girls. Autumn would stay with the family and attend a small private high school there. It seemed like a great opportunity that not many kids Autumn's age could have.

In reality, she would be turning seventeen that fall, had many friends, was riding her horse, Layla, almost daily, and was making her own money. Autumn said yes but with a bit of hesitation. Over the few months, arrangements were made, but the excitement turned to grief. At the point of departure, Autumn did not want to go but did to fulfill the commitment and make me happy. Truthfully, I didn't want her to go either. It would be four months until I saw her again, and she wasn't going just up the street. I convinced myself that it was an excellent experience for her anyway. I also knew that I would not be able to pay for Layla's boarding, food, and vet care when she was gone, so days before Autumn left, I regretfully sold the horse. Trying to make Autumn feel better, I told her we'd get another horse when she came home.

Autumn left the first part of September, so she could be there before the school year in England began. She was in a very small class, at her school, and made some special friendships right away. The two young girls she was responsible for liked her very much, as did their father. The mother, however, treated Autumn like Cinderella. In addition to taking care of the children, Autumn was told to do all sorts of other work and had to bear the brunt of the woman's bad attitude, too. I got so many calls from my daughter, pleading to come home, but I told her she needed to stick with it until Christmas.

Since Autumn was working so much for the family while in England, she didn't have the social life she'd had back in California. The British diet was much more starch ridden than what we had been eating at home, so she gained some weight as well. Typical of England, it rained almost continuously while she was there, so Autumn's usually bright positive mood slipped into a depression. Phone calls and letters came, and I can't say that I ignored them, but I didn't hear what I should have. I still feel that this time in England, for Autumn, hurt her in more ways than it expanded her worldview. I should have brought her home after the first phone call.

Autumn flew home in December just before Christmas and stayed home. She was not the same, and neither was I. I was becoming more and more swallowed up by my eating issues and constant working out, and it was affecting more than my body. Somehow, during the time she was gone, I sold Autumn's tack, including her saddle, blanket, and bridle. I don't remember selling any of it, but I do remember trying to reason with her about not getting another horse because she would be going off to college in another year. The monstrosity of a mother I was during these years still makes me shudder. I love my daughter more than life itself and would never hurt her purposely, yet my actions during this time are further proof that my body was eating itself.

We wasted no time in getting Autumn back in school at a small, fast-paced, high school called SunSet, and life returned to a so-called normal. I was still training myself and many clients. Since dating the spinning guy, I was cycling 30 miles before working out three times a week. Autumn was busy with school, work, and a new boyfriend. We'd go out for sushi occasionally. She came with me to get my belly button pierced because she'd already had one for a few years, and her senior year, we got tattoos together.

As she got older and more observant, she, along with my mom, grew worried and frustrated at my dietary choices. I would just brush it off because I saw myself doing the best things I could be doing, working out and eating healthy. The more I limited what I ate; I also was limiting what my daughter was eating. I only bought organic vegetarian and vegan groceries that included very little grains. She became a teen dealing with her own body image while I was obsessed with mine. I felt euphoric, quick and light on my feet, but improper nutrition and excessive working out, while weighing 103 pounds and having four percent body fat, will do that. More tests came back showing severe anemia and deteriorating organs. I refused to believe it was because of my diet.

Just after Autumn started her senior year in high school, I went on a hiking trip to Austria with a client friend. She flew us first class to Germany. We drove all over Austria staying mostly in bed and breakfasts along the way. We hiked what seemed like every village and part of the Alps. We explored salt mines and caves, and I got a massage and chakra reading from an old Austrian woman. As her son translated for me, the woman told me that I was severely malnourished and too thin. She said I needed fat in my diet, and her son would take us out to dinner where I would get a cream or butter based soup. We did go out with the young man, and I allowed him to order my soup. Though I was physically afraid to eat it, I also did not want to disappoint or get in trouble with any spirits. I ate half of it and all of my salad. Then, I felt like I needed to hike an extra mountain to burn the fat off.

At the end of our trip, we came back to the hotel from an all-day hike. A crowd of people was in front of a TV watching what looked to be an action film. We were walking through the lobby when a British man called out, "You American? You had better come see this!" We walked up to find the World Trade Center burning on TV. It was September 11th, 2001, and two hijacked planes had just flown into the buildings. We watched as they fell. The shaking in disbelief soon turned into major paranoia when I couldn't get a hold of Autumn who was home alone. I also tried my mother's number without avail. When I finally heard their voices, it was only to hear momentary relief as they worried about how I would get back into the country. It took a week to find my way home. Going through Munich, with airport security bolstered with military soldiers everywhere, was scary, but we finally were able to fly into San Francisco and find our way to San Diego.

Quickly forgetting the Austrian woman's chastisement, I immediately went back to my routine of eating vegetables six times a day, drinking coffee morning and afternoon, and training either myself or clients an average of six hours a day. I had no idea how emaciated I was. From eating the massive amount of vegetables, my stomach felt bloated all the time, so I felt fat despite my pencil thin yet muscular legs and no butt. I wore children's size clothing as most size 0's were too big. I still believed I looked lean and fit.

At the gym, there was a local woman who worked out for four hours with only water and then would complain that she needed to lose more weight. She had anorexia and looked like a bag of bones. The gym tried to ban her at one point, fearing she would collapse on the stair climber and die. I remember watching her in disbelief wondering how her frail looking body could even walk. I felt sorry for her, and of course, I did not see any of the similarities between the two of us. Autumn always joked that I ate like a cow, yet I didn't even catch that pun. I did eat like a cow, grazing all day on vegetables and nothing else. Only I was not a cow, and what I ate was not enough to sustain optimal health for anyone, let alone someone who was as active as I was. By April of 2002, the person I thought I had lovingly created was literally dying, and the world started to crumble around me, both inside and out.

PART TWO

Struggling To Find The Me I Should Be

My body is my temple. If I don't take care of it, where will I live?

Surprise

One afternoon in April, after training my morning clients, I was going to meet a friend for a salad at one of my favorite places. She insisted on picking me up since it was on her way to the restaurant. I hadn't eaten anything since the small breakfast I'd had that morning, so I was starving. Once in the car, she said she had to stop by her house, really quick because she forgot her purse. When we arrived, she said she had to call her mom, so I should come in. All of it seemed odd, but I didn't ask, and I followed her inside.

We entered the living room, and I found we were not alone in the house. Sitting in a circle were my daughter and my mom as well as my best friend Kat from St. Louis, Autumn's school counselor and a woman wearing a sweatshirt with the name of an eating disorder therapy group. Very gravely, I was told to sit down in the middle of the circle and asked if I knew what was going on.

Unfortunately, I'd been a part of a couple of interventions in my life already and knew this wouldn't turn out well for me. They told me just to listen. Then, I could speak. My mom pulled out a pile of letters from family members and close friends. They all said the same thing: if I didn't get help, every single one of them would part ways with me. They couldn't watch me waste away any longer. Autumn said she'd live with my mom. My friends said they'd stop hanging out with me. My family would be disappointed and distance themselves. After every shred of evidence was laid out in front of me, all I could say was, "It looks like I don't have a choice. I've got to go to rehab."

I had two hours to pack and get to the airport. Kat would fly with me to make sure I got in the van. I was hurt to think they figured I'd be a flight risk. My mom hovered over me as I began to pack. Lightheaded from not eating since that morning and still trying to wrap my head around the intervention, I asked how for how long I needed to pack. My mother laughed after I guessed two or three days. A week? Again, she said no.

I stood up and yelled, "How long? A MONTH? And what am I going to do with all of my clients?"

Very quietly, but solidly, my mom answered that my friends and clients had been notified, and other trainers at the gym were going to work with them while I was away, so I was not to worry about that. She told me that I should pack for at least three months.

THREE MONTHS?! My insides started shaking. Suddenly, I had so many questions and concerns and *anger*. Did they not know I was eating the most exceptional food available to me? Did they not *see* how strong and lean I was? Did they have to gang up on me to tell me?

I began to crumble into a river of tears. My mother left with Autumn to lessen the pain of departure. Kat helped me finish packing and drove us to the airport. I was upset, nervous and starving. We went to the bar to get a drink to slow things down. When we were in the air, I tried to eat a couple of handfuls of nuts and a few bites of the apple I brought from home. Even though my stomach pains were fiercely calling out my hunger, I just couldn't eat. It was 9 pm, and I hadn't eaten since breakfast when I was used to eating every three hours.

We landed and went to the baggage claim. Kat started crying and apologizing. As heartbroken as I was at that moment, Kat too, was feeling like a traitor as she waited for the shuttle to take me to rehab. We'd always been there for each other, and even though she knew this is what I needed, it didn't lessen the betrayal. I still didn't see the need. With non-stop tears streaming down her face, Kat closed the van door behind me and waited until I was driven away before she went back to the airport to catch her flight back to St. Louis.

I'm sure this intervention still weighs heavy on her heart. To escort your best friend to rehab, knowing what is coming, knowing somehow it is best is tough. It seemed like only yesterday we were driving across country, hauling a trailer, and hoping for a great new life for me. I don't think I can ever be grateful for what she did, but I understand that I pushed myself so hard that a few simple sentences and reoccurring medical tests obviously didn't make me see what I was doing to my body. At that moment, it felt like my life was gone. I had arrived in Hell.

Welcome To Hell

I spent the long ride to rehab doubled over in hunger and emotional pains. It was near midnight. I was shaking with fear. The minute we arrived at intake, the nurses went through my luggage like a robber tosses a house. They took everything except my clothes which they inspected, too. I asked if I could eat before I went to sleep, and harshly, the answer was no.

As I stood there numbly, the head nurse dictated from memory, "You will now eat what we give you and when we give it to you. No caffeine or chewing gum allowed, and every incoming letter or card will be checked for food items or gum."

They took my picture and weighed me. I was 94 pounds. They told me that would be the last time I could look at my weight while I was there. I was shown to bed just outside the nurse's station, in intensive care, due to my weight and being a new arrival. As tired as I was, too many emotions were thundering in time with my hunger.

I was 42 years old and in rehab because my 18 year-old daughter was worried. It turns out that Autumn had gone to her school counselor with concern for me and my weight. My daughter was taking care of me! I gave her everything I could, and she was the one who really had her stuff together. For as driven as I had been, for as keen as I was on researching food awareness, for as hard as I tried to be the greatest mother, I was failing.

They woke me up at 6 am, took my blood pressure, pulse, and weighed me again. I was told to check out my shampoo, soap, and razor from the nurse's station to take a shower before seeing the lineup of doctors they had scheduled for me later that morning. My disbelief at what someone could possibly do with these items and why I needed to be watched as I showered was met with a lecture. This first of many lectures I received expanded on the reasons why a facility like this even existed: every female here had labels such as anorexia, bulimia, cutter, alcoholic, binger or some combination therein; a razor was a danger to a cutter, and even shampoo had trace amounts of alcohol. Every action had to be watched for odd behaviors that could hinder healing. I shook my head and took my shower under the stalker eyes of an attendant.

I lined up for breakfast with ten other girls ranging from 18 to mid-50's. As I neared the front of the line, I scanned the hot tables and kitchen area. My heart plummeted. The majority of what I saw came out of a can, or a box and had undergone a fair amount of processing and was most likely bought in gigantic quantities. I passed my tray along the food buffet. A slab of chopped, formed, and processed ham was slapped onto my plate. Toasted white bread with margarine, scrambled eggs, and canned fruit cocktail followed with one cup of decaf coffee with soy milk.

When I told an attendant that I was vegan/vegetarian and allergic to wheat, I could almost hear her derision. She told me there would be no vegan option and that I could omit two food items which would be substituted for something equivalent. I chose to omit meat and dairy and pleaded no wheat. Celiac disease seemed to have no definition here because I was told I had to eat the bread anyway. At the end of the allotted 25 minutes of breakfast time, I was physically and mentally a wreck, but my schedule was booked. First, I met with a medical doctor, but after that, there was a dietician, a psychiatrist, and a dedicated psychologist/counselor.

The doctor ran a slew of tests on me, asked me too many questions, and concluded that I was pretty damn strong for someone who was supposedly anorexic. He understood my wheat allergy, so he changed my meal plan to include rice bread. He was very kind and told me that I would remain in intensive care until I started to gain weight on a regular basis. He also seemed very concerned with my gallbladder and digestion problems. With so many years of eating no or low fats, he wondered how I was even absorbing anything of what I ate and how my body would react to the new diet here.

The dietician was next. After talking with her at length about my organic food lifestyle, she said my problem was that I had become too smart about food and had put myself in such a tight bubble of veggies, fruit, and nuts that I was not getting the balanced nutrition my body needed to keep going. I ended up teaching her a few things, and she was helpful in trying to compromise and work with me. Unfortunately, I still had to eat everything I was given which was either processed, a meat substitute, soy, rice, breads, and crackers or had white sugar. In addition, I had to meet with her up to three times every week to review my diet plan. I asked her about getting out of intensive care, and she assured me that, with the vast amounts of "nutrition" they served here, most girls were out within four days.

Next, I met with the shrink. He was a quiet, reserved, compact gentleman with dark hair and glasses. At first, I was nervous, but he made me feel comfortable enough to chat with him for an hour. After he told me I was not anorexic, but rather, I had the "new eating disorder of the millennium" called orthorexia. This is given to a person who narrows down their eating choices for what they believe are health reasons but, unknowingly, put themselves at risk instead. I was told many female athletes were getting labeled with this new disorder.

Despite this fancy new word, I thought the psychiatrist was cool. He let me know he understood, yet he also had a job to do. When he stayed on campus and had dinner with us, he always sat next to me and talked about fitness and hiking. It was refreshing to know someone was on my side despite having to show me how wrong I'd been with my food choices.

Lastly, I met with my primary psychologist. She was an earthy type of woman in her 30's who seemed to want to make everything 'deeper' than it was. I think her goal was to dig and probe, to uncover everything to the point of breaking down and sobbing, or screaming. After our first conversation, she thought she had me figured out. She believed I was a high strung athlete escaping a hurtful past and pretending to be a super-charged, happy, positive woman. She figured I had control issues and had isolated myself often to avoid comments about eating habits. She was correct on some of this.

Even in my tenuous emotional state, I knew enough to say what she wanted me to say. She had paperwork to fill out, and she had the ultimate power over me while I was here. Suddenly, the realization that I had just lost control of my own life became crippling.

Break Down Or Break Free

For days, I sobbed. We were allowed ten minutes on the phone every day, and I spent every second of that calling my daughter, my mom, my dad, my grandmother, and friends begging for them to come get me. Their voices were unemotional, even robotic in response. Every single one of them told me I had to stay, that it was for the best, that they would disown me if I didn't follow through.

At one point, my legs went out from under me. I simply collapsed. I thought that this must be what it felt like to have a nervous breakdown. Just days earlier, my life was picture perfect. Now, everyone around me was telling me that I was doing it all wrong. I was stuck in a hellhole while my life continued back home *without me*. I had no say so about anything in my life. From morning, when their alarm told me to wake up, to the strictly timed breakfast, lunch, and dinner that served food fit for a truck driver, I was told what to do and when to do it.

By the third day, I surrendered. If I were to survive, I'd have to play their game. To give in meant to change my mindset and adapt to the conditions. I couldn't keep thinking that I had just lost my life. To find the positive side of having every decision taken away from me, I started looking at it as an all-inclusive vacation. Every meal was made for me, exercise (which was one-half hour of light tai chi), and other classes were routinely scheduled, and there were other girls, so I was never lonely. All I needed to do was follow along. Just smile and do.

Of course, my super-charged, happy, self got in the way, and I started looking for loopholes. I got the nurses to call my physical therapist back in Encinitas, so he could give them the exercises I was supposed to be doing for a hip injury I sustained about a month before my admission. That was 15-20 minutes of exercises and stretching I could do "legally" every day. When no one was looking, I would throw in squats, pushups, and crunches. By the time the nurses came to wake me up at 6 am, I had already done 100 crunches in bed and was pretending to be asleep again. Isometrics became my secret any-time all-time exercise because I could always tighten some muscle group for a few seconds no matter where I was.

For nearly two weeks, I continued this as I stayed in intensive care. I began to question the length of my stay near the nurse's station since I remembered the dietician saying that most girls were able to move into a room after only three or four days. The doctors admitted they were baffled because, despite the 3,000 plus calorie meal plan, I had still managed to lose weight. I had dropped to 89 pounds. On top of that, my gallbladder was distressed, and the doctor wanted to take it out.

I put my foot down. I may have had all of my other decisions stripped away from me, but I was not going to get surgery and dope myself up with pharmaceutical drugs! The doctors shook their heads and told me the only choice left was to ride it out and hope that my gallbladder would get used to the food. There were terrible pains, and I could tell my body was rebelling. Sometimes, I vomited after the enormous meals, but I kept telling myself to suspend judgment and let go.

After two weeks, my weight finally stabilized. I was told my metabolism finally flipped. My body was no longer in starvation mode. I was also able to move into my own room. This was a good day indeed! I was ecstatic about having a little privacy. Without a nurse on me 24/7, I could amp up my exercising.

Each room had two girls and a bathroom. We each had a bed and a closet. It wasn't a huge room, much like a dorm room in college, but it was more private than my previous bed that was overlooked by the nurses. I moved into the room as a single occupant, but after a week, a roommate moved in. She was a pro tennis player, so the idea of a secret workout made the hellhole a little better for her, too. The bathroom was the hidden gem of each room. That extra door made all the difference.

I would get up at 5 am, go to the bathroom and work out. Each pushup, crunch, kickback, and step up kept my sanity more intact. I'd play their eating game and eat what, when, and how they wanted me to. I'd go to all the therapy sessions and do everything they asked, but if I was going to maintain a thread of myself throughout this so-called learning process, I was going to work out. Dips, toilet step-ups, and overhead presses with my suitcase kept my body from turning to mush and flab. When I could finally go on the daily walks, I stashed rocks so I could curl with them later.

As I reveled in my secret exercises, my activity level in public view was kept to a strict minimum. Because of my low weight, I needed to stay as still as possible. I should have been walking to therapy sessions, sitting, or lying down. The nurses would even scold me for bouncing my leg under the table. I've done it unconsciously since I was young, but they said that it was burning too many calories. My psychologist went so far as to suggest I start taking a downer to get rid of some of my energy.

For as much pressure as they applied to me, I stayed positive. The younger girls began to come to me for a cheery light, anytime. Sometimes, I would share basic exercise programs with them which held the hidden excitement of something stolen and energized the overall vibe of the place. The nurses eventually chided me for being so nice and friendly. In reality, they didn't like everyone coming to me for advice instead of them. My walls were happily plastered with cards and homemade posters from friends and family. Though I was missing Easter, Mother's Day, and my birthday, I wasn't going to stay here forever, so I had to participate and make the best of a bad situation.

Dealing With Demons

*J*ust as broad as the definition is, our therapy sessions also ran the gamut from left to right. We were submitted to everything from expression through art, meditation and spirituality, to body image, biology and nutrition classes, to the dreaded support group discussions, and one-on-one sessions with the therapists. As we began, it seemed that most of the meetings were centered around the core issue of control. What was it that created either the need to control our eating or loss of control as seen in binging? Something had happened that triggered the need for or loss of control, so finding and dealing with that demon was the first step in our healing.

We were always given a few days, in advance, to write something before we had to share it. They told us to dig into our past, to look for something that caused us to feel helpless. As each of us tore into our most sensitive memories, the psychologist poked and prodded even further into our centers until rivers of tears came. All of the stories slashed straight to the core. One woman had started to starve herself at age 12 because she was never as good as her brother, according to her parents. Another's mother died, and after her father's attention was devoted to his new wife, she started cutting herself and eating jars of peanut butter with bagels. Invariably, we came together in support of our different journeys on the way to wellness.

When I was told my turn was coming, I had no clue what to write. I have always viewed my life as idyllic. As a family of six, we all loved and were loved unconditionally. We took plenty of family trips to both near and far destinations, spent summers at our lake house in Culver, and traveled to Florida where my grand-parents had a house in Key Largo. We played at the Kokomo Country Club, and we joined so many extracurricular activities that we were always on the go. Then I remembered Dr. Kindle.

I had been twelve when we stopped going to our usual church. My father had started saying things like, "Don't let anyone tell you what to believe in" and "We all must follow our hearts." We had even visited some of the other churches in town. Eventually, my dad found the meditation tapes of a popular minister who preached at the head of a nationally known, non-denominational, Christian church in Encino, California. Clifton Kindle was half Jewish, half Cherokee, taught Eastern philosophy, and was recog-nized worldwide for his meditation practices. My dad revered his work, so he began to host the minister at our house in Indiana once, sometimes twice, a year. Dr. Kindle would teach in the community and also conduct what he called energy work with his followers in our basement or their homes.

One night during one of his stays, I was laying on the couch, under a blanket in the family room, while my parents, and he were in the living room. It was late, so I was in my pajamas, and my siblings were in bed. There was a break in the discussion, and this man of supposed great Spirit came from the next room. He laid down next to me and helped himself under my blanket. I remember being confused by his intentions, but he was so familiar with our family that I was willing to take a moment and see what happened.

The sweet words that came in front of his gentle probing touch did nothing to calm my immediately pounding heart. The voices of my mom and dad were muffled in the background. I silently called to them, "Save me," but his hands continued up my shirt. He explored and fondled my developing body, my developing sense of self. His soft words were meant to caress my budding curves and make me feel special.

"Does this feel good, sweetheart?" My underpants weren't the impenetrable chastity belt hoped for by my parents. The words got dirtier, his fingers went farther. I was frozen. Tears welled up as I tried to figure out if this was a test from God. This man was invited into our home every year and mingled through the community preaching goodness, trust, and faith. His life's work was to bring meditation to thousands via stereo-taped teachings and lead workshops worldwide. This man surely had to have my parents' permission to be allowed to do this. I let him because he was a man of God, and he had been staying in our house like he was a beloved family member.

Someone suddenly got up in the other room. At that moment, he sat upright to act as if nothing happened, I bolted, needing no more of an opening. I cried all night in confusion. Early in the morning, he came into my room and kissed me salaciously.

As I was getting up to leave for school, he kissed me again. I asked my parents that night about the kisses, afraid and unsure how to even put words to what went on under the blanket. They responded that he was a loving man and was openly affectionate to all of his female followers. I felt even more confused and couldn't figure out why this vague explanation was all my parents could provide, so I just dropped it.

I had buried it. I didn't talk to anyone about any part of that night or the following morning for many years. I felt like I was the bad one, the one who should be shamed. I was afraid people would find out my shame. I feared the preacher, and though he continued to come to Indiana every year, I was never again alone in the same room with him. For a long time, I feared him in such a primal way that my insides quivered, and my heart raced. Always wanting to believe in the good of all people, I didn't question his actions or my actions or even share what happened with anyone until I was in my early 20's. I didn't tell my parents when they wanted him to be the officiant for my first wedding. The horrible act was done. Nothing could be changed. I just wanted everything to be fine.

Control

The therapist probed all the angles and brought out details that I had squashed long ago. I hadn't wanted the minister to touch me, to feel my most sensitive parts, to take a little of my innocence that night, under the blanket on the family couch, but he did do it, and I couldn't undo it. Maybe, I recognized what good he'd taught my dad and how many people looked forward to his visits. I had always wanted to see the good in people and had even worked hard since I'd been a young child to help, nurture, and make everything better.

Being the oldest of three other Blacklidge kids, I was automatically on the welcoming committee for every subsequent arrival. Right from the beginning, this gave me a sense of responsibility, and I felt quite special to help care for them. Not only was I the first child born into our family, but I was also the first grandchild. I'd always felt an expectation to set the example on how to behave and represent the family. In my mind, part of that burden dictated that things went smoothly. There was never any disappointment and rarely any guilt trips, cast upon me if expectations were not met, so it was a burden I carried enthusiastically.

From childhood well into my teens, I also cared for any help-less or injured animals I found. We lived in a brand new rural housing development, so as more houses were built, the more wild nature was being kicked out of their homes. I would find kittens in dumpsters or boxes on the side of the road and bring them home. Bunnies and even a nest of mice found their way into my infirmary. When my mom caught wind of an overflow, she'd make me give them away or release them back into the wild. I cried every time because I had named them and swore I remembered every single one of them.

When my brother was in the fifth grade, he brought home an incubator to hatch chicken eggs for a school project on parental imprinting. Our cat knocked the full incubator over and got a hold of one of the newly hatched chicks. My parents told me he wouldn't make it, but I completely disagreed. I took the injured peep and fed it chicken noodle soup, every three hours, thinking that the noodles would be like worms to the chick. The chick made it and turned into a noisy rooster that lived in our garage until it was decided he had to live in a dog house in the side yard.

Maybe, it was the two behaviors of nurturing and wanting everything to be okay that combined into my disastrous control issues. The first abusive boyfriend I had could be considered a mix of both behaviors gone wrong. Always thinking that he was truly sorry and that he had a good heart, I had been determined to help and trusted that he would change if I showed him enough love. For three years, I had stayed in that relationship before it was severed with an abortion.

Years later, after Autumn and I had moved from our funky little house in Broadripple, Indianapolis, back to Kokomo, there had been another abusive relationship. He and I had known each other for nearly eight years prior, and he'd always been wonderful. We'd been less than three months into dating seriously and living together when his jealousy and control issues surfaced. Quite suddenly, I hadn't been able to do anything without fear of getting yelled at or worse; the walls punched because I wasn't exactly as he wanted me. Still yet, I had cared so deeply for him that I waited until I was out of town to ask him to move out.

The doctors at rehab were convinced that the minister's molestation was at the root of my control issues. I had then become a victim, in at least three abusive relationships, and this repetitive cycle created my desire to be in control. I had complete control over how I trained and what I ate plus I saw the cause and effect happen in my own body which then fueled my desire for more. Eating organic foods satisfied my mother hen instinct since I was only putting good food in and taking care of myself. I alone was the master of my body, creating and sculpting it, so I felt confident that I was in complete control. Being on the podium in multiple bodybuilding competitions, only massaged the idea that I had a body everyone wanted.

To tear down the wall that I had built around the molestation experience, the psychologists made me write a letter to Dr. Kindle. They felt that confronting the offender would reinforce that it was not my actions that led to my current predicament, and it would, hopefully, help break down my need for ultimate control. I found out where Dr. Kindle lived and wrote the letter.

I put the emotional hurt back onto him, illustrated the lasting effects his actions had on me, and sent it off. Whether he ever got it or read it, I'll never know, but part of the load I carried from that fateful night was released.

The psychologist also had me reenact the couch scene, but this time as the adult there to stop him. I told Dr. Kindle that it is not okay under any circumstances to feel up a young girl. I laid out the tremendous emotional and psychological pain that had followed me and how it had been made out of a chunk of time less than 15 minutes. His quick moments of self-serving enjoyment had created years of ill health because I had tried to bury the stress of understanding. I started crying and told him I'd tried to figure out why he did it, why me, and how evil he was when he was *supposed* to be so good.

I finally understood that it had nothing to do with me. It settled in my mind that all of his "energy work" that he did in our basement or other parishioner's homes had less to do with spirituality and more to do with a small-town's boredom that played into an easily hid excuse for adultery and pedophilia. I was, at once, sickened but also released from the weighty questions that I'd pretended hadn't plagued me since the night it happened.

Visions

During my time in rehab, there were three other significant experiences to come out of therapy that had lasting effects on my future self. Though I spent much of my time handing out mini workouts and readjusting my mindset making rehab a much-needed vacation, I also wanted to make sure I learned what I could from this hellhole of an experience. I was not going to let stolen rocks be the mascot of my stay here.

Once a week, a nun would come in to discuss the 12 steps, share spirituality, and lead meditation exercises. It was during one of the meditation times that my past came back to me in full force. We were all lying on the floor, the room was dark, and a beautiful meditation tape was playing. There were sounds of nature and gentle waves rolling on a beach, a gentle voice guided us further into relaxation, and then it went back to peaceful calming sounds of nature. I closed my eyes, relaxed fully, and just cleared my mind to a state where I just *was*. Nothing was polluting my thoughts. My breathing was calm and my body was simply a body.

Suddenly, I saw myself. I was lying down with my arms over my chest when a tall, dark shadow slowly came forward. I felt this figure was male, had great power, and was beyond wise. He came to my side, and I heard him speak though there was no sound. He spoke with his mind and heart. I heard as well as felt him. Without any doubt, in my mind, I knew it was my grandfather who had passed away almost ten years prior. He had been a great man and even in this simple state of being; he held my undivided attention.

While on this earth, he and I had been very close. Being his firstborn grandchild, I had held a special place in his heart. Our birthdays were just two days apart, and we were similar in demeanor, attitude, and so much more. He had been senior jerk to my junior jerk, our inside joke.

His shadowy apparition held out an upturned hand, demanding me to stop. In a non-verbal but unequivocal voice, he said, "You little jerk. You know what you are doing, and you must stop it! I love you very much, and you need to stay." His words came to a close, and his dark figure faded into the blackness of my being as another soft, white entity slowly approached.

This silky silhouette portrayed a female spirit, and she laid a gauzy hand on my heart. In the same unspoken way, she soothed, "I love you, and you are going to make it through this and be fine." This soul kissed my soul as she faded into nothingness. I knew this was my maternal grandmother who had always been the epitome of unconditional love. She had passed away from cancer sixteen years earlier.

I did not feel the tears streaming down my face. To have the two most influential people in my life visit in my darkest time was both crippling and uplifting. I missed both of them more than I could ever explain, and here they were, telling me to quit this shit and that everything was going to be okay. Just as when they were living, they commanded me to be smarter than my actions yet caressed my aching soul.

Worried and standing over me, the nun leading the exercise shook me out of this dream state. She asked me to share what I could of this experience and then to further explore it through art and journaling. Her attempt to forge this in my memory forever was feeble. It was already seared into my being. Having my most inspirational elders come and touch my soul wasn't something that I could have orchestrated nor was it something that I could forget. Ever.

Another exercise that genuinely illustrated the dichotomy of my eating disorder was a letter I had to write to my own body. After working on our letters, we had to read them aloud to the group. Mine was nothing like the other girl's letters. Words full of hate and unhappiness filled the room as they read their letters, each coloring specific body parts with words like fat and ugly. My letter was the opposite:

Dear Body of Mine,

This is my Body Temple.

You have been the house that Spirit and I have lived in for 43 years now. You have held tight through ups and downs and sickness and health... remained my pillar of strength and firm foundation... you are my space suit for my Spirit.

I built your structure up strong... brick by brick... muscle by muscle. I loved the exterior beauty of my craftsmanship.

Somewhere along the way, in the midst of all this ongoing tearing down and building up, I neglected to care for your internal structure. Spirit kept telling me, sometimes even screaming at me to not neglect what lies beneath the structure. A little interior decorating and caring for was in dire need. External voices propelled me to continue to ignore Spirit's voice and continue to build and tear your external walls to the point of serious damage. Your inside was crumbling while the external structure was now starting to deteriorate. What was happening? I (mind) was screaming that everything was fine; just a minor relapse in construction work while Spirit is crying... Are you in self-destruct mode? If so, where will I live? If you do not start rebuilding now, from the inside out, my house will fall, and I will have no home. (Your physical body will die).

Begin with a strong foundation first. Then, you may beautify the external surface. Spirit loves this house. I love this house. I am so very sorry I have deafened my ears to Spirit's powerful, loving patient voice. It is the voices from outside... from my loved ones that gave you this new structure... my now body. They gave you the saving push to get help. I resisted but knew I had to rebuild or my home would crumble soon.

In the midst of rebuilding, I must accept and welcome the new design which may be quite different from the one I have become accustomed. Parts of the external house will grow and be built faster than others, and until the entire home is completed and all is buffed out and distributed as it should be, I may get frustrated or disappointed at times at the imbalances. With Spirit's voice and patience, I know the finished project will be a beautiful piece of work architecturally inside and out. Strong, balanced, and ready to house Spirit and me for the next 43 years... with the course, I will accept the expected and welcomed ongoing changes throughout time and the maturing of you... my precious-unique home.

My body is my temple (my home). If I don't take care of it, where will I live?

I respect my body temple.

~ Written by Dawn Blacklidge on May 29, 2002

Silence filled the room after my reading. It was all there, spelled out between the lines: I wasn't here because I hated my body. I was here because I had become so focused on creating a perfect body that I had neglected to follow basic nutritional needs. I didn't eat wheat because I was allergic. I didn't eat red meat because corporations had taken empathy out of the process. I didn't eat dairy because of Autumn's infections and congestion. I didn't eat fat or sugar because of the unhealthy implications. The list went on, and every reason was a legitimate reason, but when combined all at once for a long time, it meant disaster. My body had been living off of vegetables and protein from nuts and legumes for too long. There wasn't any base upon which to sustain my organs much less to sustain my body or mind.

This exercise helped me realize two things: I did love myself/ my body, and I didn't want to die. I may have been admitted into rehab against my will, but I understood the strain and worry those close to me had harbored for the last few years. For quite some time, the doctor's tests had been showing me the results of my extreme dieting, yet I saw them all as viral or bacterial rather than symptoms of the whole breaking down. I didn't want to see the big picture because I alone had created the reflection in the mirror. I liked what I saw because I had done it, and the image of muscular and lean was stroked by people I admired. Though I take full blame for my actions, I can see that many small instances built upon another to manipulate my mind. It is a powerful thing to pick and choose paths in our lives while, at the same time, being influenced by the thoughts of others who are just as lost in this thing called life.

The last exercise that helped to carve the way for my future was a dream board. We had to make a big collage of where we saw ourselves or where we wanted to be in five years. I cut out a picture of a tropical island and surrounded it with a fit and healthy woman, loving family members, and a mate to share a wonderful life with while in paradise. My focus was optimal health and fitness. My daughter would be happy and healthy, and the rest of my family would continue to nurture close, loving relationships with each other. This was an uplifting experience for all of us because it showed a light when we were still mingling with demons.

The Mistress

Rehab isn't a place anyone wants to be. It demands confronting your damaging self and attempting to rise above it all, hoping that the new self will remain who you are yet without all the bad stuff. It is a lot of work on many levels. Obviously, therapy tore us all down past the breaking point of crying, screaming, and hating then tried to rebuild us in a sturdier, better fashion. The mindset that I also had rearranged within my brain, just to survive rehab was something I never hope to experience again. Making a place that exposed everything bad about me into a vacation, from myself, was an Athenian feat. Although, it did further support the idea that a mindset can be a promoter for the positive. Grappling with the time spent there, while for the rest, life is somewhere else, was perhaps the most heart wrenching of all. To realize that I messed up, so much, that I was actually in rehab, rather than spending time with family and friends, made that quick trip into Starbucks, to get coffee, when you're late already, an experience I was missing. I was longing for the routines of my everyday life.

After missing the most meaningful celebrations in the spring, including Mother's Day and my birthday, I wasn't about to miss my daughter's graduation. I had been in rehab for ten weeks and now weighed 106 pounds. From weighing 89 pounds, a week after admission, to 106 pounds, I felt great. My body was not bony anymore. I had a little cushion, but I still had muscle tone which I greatly appreciated. Unfortunately, the dietician had set my 'safe weight' at 108 pounds, so I could not graduate and leave until I gained those last two pounds. Another stipulation of graduation was the mandatory donation of my "skinny jeans" to Goodwill. I scoffed at that. My jeans had cost $160, and I loved them! I hid them even if they were getting a bit snug.

I begged my mom and daughter not to be disappointed and think I was a failure because I didn't complete the entire process, but I was not going to be absent from my only daughter's biggest day. Knowing and seeing how much work I'd put into myself, they told me they were incredibly proud and wouldn't hold anything against me.

I began to make preparations for my departure. Though I was going to leave against their recommendation, my final group therapy session was set. I was to have the most important and influential people in my life with me. I asked my mother, my daughter, and my father. My mom and daughter had always been there for me, and they were honored to participate. My dad said he would have to decline unless he could bring his wife. I felt his wife had no place in my process, so I asked again if he would come without his wife. He declined. This emotionally cutting act broke my heart. His wife now came before anyone else, even when one of his kids needed him.

This separation from his original family, unless his new wife was included, had been becoming more of a monster in the room than any elephant. From my very first meeting with this woman, I'd felt uneasy and suspicious of an underlying motive and a heavy-handed purposeful manipulation from her. She had come to our house when my parents were still together, and I was in high school. My dad had said he'd met a new employee at the Crisis Hotline in Kokomo who'd just moved into town with her small child. She had been a Purdue graduate and was a gymnastics coach. Since my gymnastics coach had just said I was so advanced she couldn't teach me anymore, I remember being excited to meet her. My dad had invited her over to dinner.

This woman arrived with her toddler daughter who was sleeping, so we immediately led her to my room so the little one could continue her nap. I remember seeing the girl's cherubic face. The woman was white, but the child was half African American. Her dark chocolate skin was made even more striking by the bright, sunshine yellow snowsuit she wore. I suddenly understood my father's generosity to this unknown, recently transplanted woman. She was a single mother of a mixed race child in small-town, conservative Kokomo, Indiana. Indeed, one might have a hard time making friends.

Regrettably, her energy did not match the excitement I had to meet her. She was uncomfortable to be around and was not friendly to the rest of my family. She and my father immediately disappeared into the living room while my mother was busy making dinner in the kitchen. Not once, during the time she was in the house, did she offer to lift a finger in assistance. Self-centered and ungrateful are words that ring mercilessly in my head, even today. I had uneasy feelings, yet was willing to give my dad the benefit of the doubt that he'd never cheat on mom, and he was just the compassionate guy I knew him to be. She was only in need of friends, plus she could help me with gymnastics.

Over the next few years, my dad seemed to take himself away from us more and more. He was working on his second Master's degree, so he took an apartment in town to find the quiet needed to study (so he said). Also, being an incredible hobbyist photographer, he converted one of the rooms in the apartment to a dark room. By escaping our noisy house for poring over library books and developing photos, our family time together was crumbling. My mother hid so much from us. She maintained that she had the four most perfect reasons to protect from anything damaging to our unit.

My parents never missed a gymnastics meet, football game, or any other activity of their children. My dad and this new friend soon started coming together to our activities and sitting away from my mom. I would occasionally see her car drive by our house though her house was across town. It was always at odd hours, much like the phone calls that would ring in our house that were disconnected when we picked up. One night she called hysterical, claiming there was a bat in her house, and Dad had to take care of it. My dad was in bed with his wife, yet he got up and went off as a knight on a mission, in the dark, to save a damsel in distress.

Was he simply being a Good Samaritan? Or was he a heartless, cheating man? My sister questioned the growing time away from our family but ultimately pushed it aside. My youngest brother was probably too young to put it all together, but I suspect my other brother was beginning to see how lame and weak his actions were. Perhaps, the most naïve of all, I chose to believe he was helping a scared, young, single mom. I wanted to see the best in everyone, assuming that everything was well and good.

After high school graduation and working for a year while living at home, I broke the news to my mom that I would be moving into a place with abusive boyfriend #1. To this day, her words are imprinted in my ears: "Oh, great, and your father just told me he is leaving, too!"

For years, I should have known, but I just didn't want to see the truth. I loved my dad so much and thought he was such a hero. I couldn't wrap my head around his new lady friend being anything more than a family friend. The time she stole my dad had slowly but irretrievably been growing larger. It was the greatest scheme a con ever played, and my dad, somehow unhappy in his life with a wife and four kids, willingly let himself be led straight into it.

When I was 22, I finally broke the silence, to my sister, about Dr. Kindle and the couch at a huge family BBQ hosted by my grandparents. As I recounted this horrific experience, dad's girlfriend walked into the room. She grabbed onto the drama of the situation and threw it into my dad's face. Being a counselor, she demanded we have a family meeting about it.

Days later at my dad's house, she used the time to yell at my dad, making it all his fault that it happened, and furthermore, his fault for not recognizing what had happened. My dad hung his head in defeat. Not only had he just found out that the minister he revered just molested his daughter, but he also had to face the disgraceful show his girlfriend produced to pile the blame of someone else's actions towards him.

I hurled his hurt and mine onto her and demanded the meeting be over. This was not her issue, and if it was, this was not the way I wanted to deal with it. Discussion over.

My dad was there at times that I needed him. He always helped me with a place to stay throughout my years of college and pregnancy and moving. The love that he showed Autumn was insurmountable. He was there for many Daddy-Daughter days with his granddaughter until his girlfriend inserted her claws into that relationship, too. Suddenly, he was spending too much time with Autumn. If he were carrying her as a toddler, this evil woman, posing as a thoughtful, careful girlfriend would remind him how heavy she was getting and make moves to remove the weight. Thus, she created space between my father and anyone else but her.

When Autumn was two, my dad married his adulteress girlfriend. Two of my siblings refused to attend the wedding, and I expressed reservations until my grandmother pressed. She pointed out that no matter how much any of us disliked this woman and didn't want her in the family, she was whom my father had picked, and we needed to honor that. Begrudgingly, I attended as a sole support of my father though I did not approve of the marriage.

My dad passed me his special gold turtle necklace along with a letter, as he tucked me into my new truck, hitched up to a trailer, full of my life on our way to California, I still loved him beyond measure. No matter what tangled web of deceit he had accepted with this woman, he was still my father. When I finally opened the letter after my California arrival, I knew I could never give up on my dad. He wrote:

Dear Dawn,

I am writing this on Sunday evening after you and Autumn spent the day and night with us. I can't begin to put into words how important that was to me.

I must admit I have a real hard time when allowing myself to think about the two of you being so far away from me. I know, as you said, we did not see each other all that much but just having you guys close felt good to me. I guess I'm not bad at handling 50 miles or so. Even your brother is too far.

I get pretty nostalgic if I allow myself to think of my children... and their growing up years. For some reason, your love and care for the chicken that was hurt always comes to mind.

I want more than anything for you to find your way on the path that is right for you. I know you are very sensitive and deeply spiritual and that those qualities will carry you onward to new things. I know you look forward to California with excitement, anticipation, and maybe some anxiety. Having your mom there and some old family friends should help. You will do well and feel secure again soon... as will Autumn. This is good.

I want to give you something that is special to me. I have chosen the little sea turtle from my necklace. The little guy keeps on going until she finds a home in the sea where she grows and is happy. Keep her close to your heart... For us. OK?!

I love you more than you know, Dawn. My prayers will
always be with you, and I hope you will feel that love around
you especially if you are feeling a little anxiety or uncertainty.
Good journey and God's speed.
Love you, Pop.

I've always maintained that we have a special bond, and his words
here were the truth. Even today, I have the necklace and have
saved the letter because it reminds me of the best of my dad.

In the spring of 1998, my nephew and niece were to be baptized in Kokomo. It was a big homecoming, and most of us were
very excited to share the moment. At some point during the planning, my dad approached my sister and asked if his wife's granddaughter could be baptized with the other two grandchildren. My
sister said no and tried to explain. This was to be a gathering of
siblings and loving family members to baptize two of the children
of the Blacklidge line at our grandmother's church. We did not
harbor any resentment or ill will toward his wife's daughter, but
we'd had minimal contact with her over the years, so we felt no
real connection with her. Since we wanted the experience to be
more intimate than icy, his wife's attempt to rudely insert herself
into Blacklidge family proceedings would be dismissed. To us, it
was evident that this request came from his wife rather than the
daughter.

This behavior seemed typical of her. Instead of talking to us
like real people, she commanded Dad to ask for our favor, yet did
nothing to win us over. It seemed as if she'd found a fool to do

her bidding and commanded that fool to curry love from those she desired, much like an evil queen demands respect though she gives nothing in return. When my brother arrived at their house one day to find Dad, on the bed, and his wife literally beating him as he lay there, we decided that an intervention was necessary.

The four of us siblings showed up unannounced while we were all still in Kokomo for the baptisms. We asked the wife to kindly leave the room though we all knew she would lurk just behind the closed door. We all sat together, and each of us went through how much we loved him but couldn't stand to see him slipping away. He'd always been such an extraordinary man and father, one time even driving from Florida to Indiana and back again to reunite our family for vacation after my sister and I had to stay behind for school. I broke my arm. Even though Grandma told me not to tell him, when he called, I did. This prompted him to come and get us for the remainder of the vacation.

Now, this woman had come into his life and began to orchestrate his actions like a marionette and its master. She had slowly, but deliberately, created a wedge between him and the rest of the Blacklidge family and then demanded that she be a part of it all. How could she expect acceptance from us when we felt nothing but disdain *from* her towards us? He had unwittingly become a pawn in her quest for control.

We'd all had tears and were emotionally tied together as we'd sat in his house. Though he was crying, too, all he'd said was that he'd consider everything. He hadn't publicly shown his face at the baptism, but I had seen him sneak onto the balcony alone for a bit. He also had not shown up at his mother's house for the family celebration afterward. Our breath and tears seemed in vain as he showed us once again that the only person in his life that truly mattered was his controlling and brilliantly manipulative wife.

As I sat in rehab knowing that my dad wouldn't come, I felt robbed of a father again. I still wanted to believe the best of him, but it was getting harder to love him through a wall of someone else's deceit.

Going Home

To be released from rehab, I needed to attend a family counseling session and one last private session with my psychologist. After more than two months away from my family and friends, I was ready to go. My friends and clients back at home had sent me so many cards, pictures, and care packages that I knew I had been missed. Hearing that I would be leaving without rehab's full approval was sad news, but Autumn's graduation and the lure of my own life back home were enough to cement my decision to leave with or without official completion of the program.

During the required family counseling session, my mom, daughter and I each had to draw a picture of how we all saw me before rehab and now. My picture had a rainbow and dying flowers on one side and brightly colored flowers and grass flourishing on the other side. Though it portrayed a rainbow and flowers for my pre-rehab days, it was colored in drab muted colors and showed how my mental state had made everything seem perfect. The truth was I had been slowly inching toward death. I was grateful to be able to see the end of my rehab days and the work I'd done was obvious from the well-nourished variety of thick flowers and bright green grass drawn on the opposite side.

My mom's picture started as a sunset that turned into a sunrise by the opposite end of the page. Sunsets, though they can be beautiful, signify an end whether it be the ending of the day or the much broader end of life. A sunrise is the beckoning of a new day and new beginnings. A beautiful woman was on the sunrise side, her arms wide open, praying and accepting the arrival of the dawn.

As we shared our pictures and our feelings, I was struck once again with how helpless I had made those around me feel. I may have felt empowered and in control, but everyone else saw me on a one-way path headed for a destruction of my own doing. How frustrated, angry, helpless, and heartbroken they felt, and I had to listen to it one more time. Making amends, recognizing that my behavior does affect those around me, coming to terms and accepting my wrongdoing are all different ways to say I fucked up. It was hard to hear again.

The therapist brought out my issues of control and how it may have all started with Dr. Kindle's molestation followed by abusive and continually disappointing relationships throughout my life. Just as much as I wanted Dr. Kindle's actions to go away, I wanted to be done ripping myself out of myself. I had fulfilled every medical fantasy this facility could throw at me. I had kept my sanity by keeping the flab away but enough with the feelings. How many times had I heard, "And how did that make you feel?" How many times had my answers not been good enough and had to be probed deeper?

Before my mom and daughter left, we got to go to a restaurant for dinner. Though it was a test to make sure I could and would order and eat properly, I was overjoyed to be in the company of the two closest women in my life. We talked like schoolgirls. Autumn's graduation was just days away, and we started talking about plans for the upcoming summer. The talk was light; food was eaten, and, though we all breathed with relief, they went home to San Diego while I had to stay a couple more days in rehab.

Much of my last session with my counselor was spent talking about how deeply intertwined Autumn and I were. It had been just the two of us for the last 18 years, and I had managed to wrap much of myself and my identity around her. With her graduating and the possibility of her leaving for college, the counselor was worried I would relapse. Autumn would be moving on with her life. I would be left behind. She talked about ways to sidestep little impulses but also how to stay focused. She impressed upon me that I would need to rebuild my identity as my own. Then she said that I was not to be released, but they couldn't hold me unwillingly. I was free to leave, but I would not be receiving the 12-Step Program Serenity Coin nor would I get a ride to the airport.

Good riddance is what I felt. I cheerily set about packing. Later that night, a nurse I had developed a strong bond with snuck into my room and slipped me the coin. She said more than anyone she'd seen go through the program; I deserved the coin. Another woman was being released the same day as I signed my papers, and her father generously offered me a ride. Luck be a lady, I was on my way.

At the airport, I bought my ticket and went straight to Starbucks for real coffee. We hadn't been allowed real coffee in rehab because the caffeine is a stimulant and speeds up metabolism. This first coffee in ten weeks was liquid gold. In the air, flying fast and far away from that hellhole called rehab, I felt alive. It was a bit of a culture shock to suddenly have to make every single decision after coming from a place that told me everything I needed to know and do, but I was on my own and free!

I got home the day before Autumn's graduation.

Letting Go

For quite some time after my return, I was watched like a hawk not only by my mom and daughter but also my friends and clients. The dietician from rehab had helped me set up a diet plan, and a "feelings check" network to make sure I had support if I started to slump back into hard training and selective eating. My mom was my network, but the diet plan was based on the USDA standard food pyramid which was heavy on carbohydrates. This was against all of the research I'd done about food, so I found a nutritionist in LaCosta to satisfy my mom's worry and my promise to eat. She was also a vegetarian and a Reiki healer as well, so the care in which she looked at my body and health as a whole was more aligned with what I believed.

Over the next few months, we met every week so she could weigh me and talk about my food choices which I tracked carefully. We both agreed on bypassing the USDA food pyramid because of the propensity of processed, non-organic foods that contained simple sugars. We talked about healthy, vegetarian options and how I could eat fewer carbohydrates, still be grain-free but add more good fats. My weight went from 106.5 pounds upon returning home to stable 112 pounds. My body seemed most comfortable and healthy at this weight, and I retained a right amount of muscle mass. I was eating well, gaining weight, and I was doing it my way.

I went right back to work. I was anxious and nervous, feeling like there would be many eyes on me but my clients were ecstatic to see me. They all said I looked great and that was good to hear. None of them questioned my experience which was nice because I didn't have to recount tales of rehab in a place where everyone is just trying to get fit. I did have to wonder if they were afraid I'd regress, but no matter, it was nice to be welcomed back.

Autumn attended a local community college and worked several jobs. Like before, we didn't spend much time together, but I loved knowing she was still home with me. She got a black cat and named it Zorro, then talked me into going to the Humane Society. "Just to look," she had said.

It was heartbreaking for both of us to see so many dogs locked up and crying in cages. We spent some time looking and talking with the dogs. Autumn liked a cute pit bull mix, but I kept going. The last cage I came to was huge and in it was a small quivering puppy. She was a new admission and was absolutely terrified. Autumn and I asked to take her out of the cage, so we could spend a bit of time with her. The little pup was black with brown markings and had a little white puff on her chest. She was immediately grateful for the love we offered. We knew she was the one.

We named her Jade for the rough start to life she'd had. Autumn signed her up for obedience classes and hired a doggie babysitter to come once a week to take her in a van with other puppies to socialize, run, and have fun. Even I pitched in and walked Jade when I was home, and Autumn was out. Jade provided a bit of happiness and cohesiveness to our family while we adjusted to life again.

Almost exactly a year later, Autumn dropped a bomb. She would be leaving California for college on the East Coast. Florida Atlantic University was very close to where my sister lived with her husband. Autumn could stay with them in their big house while commuting to college. She was almost 20 and very independent, but none of that made me any more comfortable with the fact she would be leaving. And not leaving for a camp or a study exchange program, but for real leaving.

We had much to do to prepare her for leaving. I went through the motions, but it was hard trying to be excited. I had to figure she was tired of living with her self-absorbed mother, but I said nothing about it. I wasn't emaciated anymore, but I was still food-focused and training like an animal. Maybe, if I would have said something, it would have been better for both of us, but I wanted to show her support.

In the midst of packing and not dealing with my emotions, a thick letter arrived from my dad. It was very long and typed out, surrounding it with an even more formal air. I had just started to read it when my mother called and told me to burn it. She, along with each of my siblings, had received the same letter. I did burn it because I had already read enough to get the tone.

In the letter, my dad lashed out and bashed every one of us, but especially Mom. The letter was so angry. From what I'd read and the bits and pieces the rest of my family told me, it stated that the 20 years he'd been married to Mom were the worst years of his life, and he just wanted to forget them. For pages, he ranted with words of hatred and disgust towards us. It was like a knife through my heart to hear our once loving father say that the time he spent involved in our childhoods were so horrible. My mom and siblings were devastated, but we had to think that these hurtful, mean things didn't start with him. He had always been the most wonderful and loving man until his new wife had entered the picture. Since that letter, there have been several more. All of them place blame on our mother AND his own mother. He was choosing to forget that time in his life when we were all young and a growing, seemingly, happy family unit.

We were in shock, confused, and hurt to think he wanted to erase all of our family trips, learning lessons, and cuddle times. We were angry to hear how badly he spoke about our mother, the woman who had stood by us faithfully as he distanced himself for years right under our noses. My mom was stunned to think that he could have been so unhappy while making and raising our family. We had to think that his new mate was behind this. Perhaps, she was left out at a family function, and this was the way she dealt with it: by making everyone else around her as hurt and angry as she was. This just added to the dislike we already had toward this woman.

Finally, my dad called me himself. I told him that I did not read his letter and tried to act like nothing was the matter. Maybe, I was still hoping to continue a loving relationship with him. I felt like I loved him more than any daughter could. Despite the loss of his support in these last few years, he was the only father I'd have, and I couldn't just toss aside the happy times I'd had with him. I dislike confrontation, so I pushed aside the whole subject of the letter. I did not want to believe he could write such cruel words and feel so much hate in his heart towards his own family.

Despite this setback with my father, life went on. I had to prepare for both Autumn's and my departures from California. Since Autumn was leaving, I decided I was going to go home to Kokomo. I would be closer to my brothers' families, my grandmother, and, yes, my dad. I would be leaving my mom, but she had a full life with her husband and group of friends. The added support and familiarity of my hometown would hopefully alleviate the feelings of loneliness that had started to set in.

I put our townhouse on the market. Luckily, it was a great time to sell. The sale was quick, and we made a good profit. Just as the townhouse was selling, I got served with papers. I was being sued by the girl who had purchased our old sunflower and eyeball condo. She claimed that I knew I was selling her a unit that had toxic black mold, and I didn't properly disclose just how much damage there had been from the flood. Basically, she had gotten sick and missed work, so someone was going to pay.

It was true that I had been told there was flooding but not to the extent she was claiming. It turns out, the Homeowner's Association for the old condo had gutted the entire place and had to rebuild it due to the extensive water damage. I'd had a couple of bouts with lung infections while I'd lived there but had never thought to dig deeper to find out why because I'd had so many other sicknesses that were connected to my overall health during that time. I was saddened by the fact that it was her word against mine, so I contacted a lawyer.

Angela had hired the most aggressive and powerful attorney in San Diego. It was obvious she had money and wanted more. I found an attorney who told me I was also due money for improper disclosure of the flooding and that I should countersue. I followed his lead because I hadn't been told the true nature of how severe the flooding was and didn't think all of the blame should fall on me. I paid thousands of dollars to the attorney only to lose the case and be ordered to pay an additional $20,000. The attorney still thought I should countersue, but I could no longer afford him and just wanted the whole thing to be over.

After a decade-long absence, I went home to Kokomo to start over.

Hometown Living

I lived in my brother's basement until I found a house. His home was luxurious, so the basement was like an apartment. It even had an exercise room! Because of his family's generous offer, I helped them with their young children, ages two and just a couple of months.

I rode my bike in the country almost daily and exercised in his weight room. I didn't want to bother anyone too much or be an imposition, so I mostly kept to myself. It felt great to be back home, and I was grateful for the support of those around me.

Despite the hateful words he had written, my dad went with me as I hunted for houses. He was very caring and showed nothing but love to me when we were alone. Since I was still trying so desperately to hang onto the dad I had grown up with; I cherished each quiet moment we had. When he wasn't around his wife, he was that dad I loved and respected, but she was very demanding and always seemed to want more of his time.

We found a house for sale across the alley from his house. The previous owner had died, and the house was just left empty. Upon opening it up, we were hit by the horrendous smell of death, smoke-stained walls, and neglect, but I loved the floor plan and the area of town. The Silk Stocking District was made up of older homes that were very nice and well-kept. I put in an offer and waited.

After the sale went through, the daunting task of renovations began. I tore out everything old. I repainted the entire house, bought new fixtures, put in French doors, and a hot tub. By the time I moved in a few months later, I had a new two bedroom, two bath, 1280 square foot house with a yard, and garage of my own. All the work kept me busy, so I would not think so much about how I missed my girl.

It was wintertime, and my tiny body shook constantly trying to stay warm. I felt sad, lonely, and out of place. I exercised at least an hour every day, worked on the house a bit, became a "power seller" on E-bay to make extra money, and began researching the new raw vegan movement on the Internet. I was immediately drawn to its claims of how healthy and cleansing it was and how it could cure terrible diseases like diabetes and some cancers.

I joined vegan singles sites, bought some raw vegan cookbooks, and began experimenting with recipes. I was so enamored with this new way to prepare food that I brought a raw 'salmon' loaf to Thanksgiving that was made mostly from almonds and carrots with some dulse and kelp to give it that ocean taste. Those that did try it said that it was pretty good.

My friends and family were very accepting of what they probably saw as my crazy ideas. Kokomo isn't a place that changes very much or very fast, so for many, the lifestyle I had chosen seemed a little too far-fetched. Those who knew me tried my food concoctions. I appreciated them greatly.

My dad was a godsend during these times. He came over every morning to make sure I was warm enough. He'd start up the truck he'd loaned me, so it was warm when I got in it. I even thought, for a minute, that I could live next to him and his wife for many years to come.

During renovations, his wife had helped me a great deal with cleaning and getting it ready to move in, so I reached out to her in the name of friendship. Sooner than I could say, "I told you so," she accused me of stealing her jewelry and told me I was not welcome to visit anytime I wanted. I was disgusted. First of all, I am not a thief, and second, I don't even wear jewelry. To have her be so underhanded just reiterated to me how manipulative she was. For every nice word that left her lips, there was an ulterior motive behind it.

Though I'd only been in Kokomo for a few months, I was paying almost $200 a month in heating costs. I was losing weight again. Between the stress of Autumn leaving, the toxic black mold lawsuit, moving, buying and remodeling a home and the frigid cold, I had lost about six pounds and was slipping back into my limited eating mode.

While I'd been living in my brother's basement, I began thinking that I wanted to live somewhere and experience something entirely outside my comfort zone. I wanted this place to be far away, somewhere tropical since I'd been shivering the entire time I'd been in Indiana, and I wanted to go for at least three months. Now that I was as comfortable as I was going to get in my new house, I started looking at options.

There were many work/trade opportunities as well as volunteer gigs called WWOOF (World Wide Opportunities on Organic Farms). I quickly found a place in Costa Rica that sounded amazing. I called the owner and bought a plane ticket. When I was just days away from leaving, my sister called me in a panic. She'd been having recurring dreams of me going to Costa Rica and dying there. I canceled everything and started looking again. That's when I found Yoga Oasis on the Big Island of Hawaii.

Yoga Oasis is a 26-acre yoga retreat nestled in the jungle between the ocean and a funky little town called Pahoa. It runs on solar, so there is no TV, and lights out is at 7 pm. There is one main shared bathroom. Peeing at night consisted of peeing in a bucket unless I wanted to foray into the night and risk bumping into someone else. I wouldn't have a car, but I could hitchhike or ride my bike. I was applying to be the raw food chef and fitness trainer for at least three months.

I called the owner, Sapphire, and sent off my resume. She asked for multiple references, which I gave confidently, and within days, I had a new job. I was very excited to embark on this new adventure. I was down to 105 pounds and shivering constantly, so I figured I'd go to Hawaii for this job and then return to Kokomo to start up my life in the conservative Midwest.

Before I left for Hawaii, my mom and grandma took me to lunch at a local diner called Jamie's. As we were eating, a woman approached the table and asked if I was Dawn Blacklidge? She wanted to know, did I teach autistic children at Petit Park school years ago? I said "yes." She broke down and cried telling me she was Tyler's mom and handed me a picture of her now 22-year-old son. She said I changed his life, and she thought he would be doomed to living in an institution, but he is now living a productive life in a group home. My heart melted. I still, today, have a photo of him and me from when he was 5-years-old. *I did make a difference.*

Welcome To The Jungle

*C*arly in January of 2004, I left Indiana on a plane bound for Hilo, Hawaii. I had two big bags, a huge backpack and my bike which was broken down and packed in a box. Though I told my family and friends I'd be back in three months; I flew on a one-way ticket just in case I had to leave earlier or wanted to stay longer. I was excited about this outside the box adventure. A sense of surging electricity followed me through my connections. I knew I was prepared enough for almost anything that met me on the other side.

Landing in Honolulu was like entering into a dream. The smell of flowers lifted me off the plane instead of cigarette smoke like most airports. There was a bus to connecting flights. I chose to walk. The way was bordered with flowers, trees, and sunshine. My short hopper flight to the Big Island wasn't until the next day, so I slept on my bike box inside the airport. Without even landing at my final destination, I felt like this was where I was meant to be.

Hansen, co-owner and head yoga instructor of Yoga Oasis, met me at the airport in Hilo with an old pickup truck. The man looked like Gandhi to me. He had dark suntanned skin, a slick bald head that took sheen from the sun, and was very lean and muscular. Words that left his mouth were soft but carried an intensity that made him seem wise beyond his years. I was in awe for the second time that day.

We threw my bags and boxed bike into the back of the pickup and headed out. Hansen said he had a few errands to run. After traveling for 20 hours, I was exhausted, but with the excitement of landing and meeting a wise man, I was happy to travel to the end of the world if that's what was on the agenda.

Travel to the end of the world, indeed. It was a 40-minute ride to Yoga Oasis from the airport. My eyes were big as I soaked in as much as I could. The foliage was so green it nearly hurt my eyes. There were no freeways and only a two-lane road going into and out of Pahoa. The closer we got, the fewer roads, buildings and houses we saw.

Pahoa itself was tiny. The one road was lined with a post office, a family-owned gas station, two small banks, a health food store, and a convenience store. Downtown was made up of a few restaurants and cute, colorful shops squished together to form a boardwalk, and there was an elementary and high school at the end of town. There were no fast food joints, no big department stores and nothing modern about this town as far as I could see. I thought I'd just landed in Heaven.

Just out of Pahoa, we drove down a small road underneath trees that were so big and lush they formed a tunnel. Lush does not describe the growth that was all around. There were beautiful tropical trees, bamboo, palms, fruiting trees, and flowers everywhere. As we drove, Hansen was telling me why he had chosen this area to build his sacred yoga retreat.

The winds, ocean, trees, and airflow combined here in the district of Puna to create the best air and oxygen quality in the world. He had found this large tract of land after much research and started planting. We turned onto a skinny, single-lane paved road. It was rough but was lined with bamboo and palms, giving way to fruit trees as we neared the main building. Just the smell of everything green was enough to make me fall in love, but combined with the sight of such abundance nearly made me swoon.

The pickup truck stopped, and we got out. A woman with a beautiful aura descended the stairs with open arms and a gentle smile. This was Sapphire, and seeing her gave me complete assurance that I had made the right choice. Looking around, I was in awe.

This place was built within nature and out of nature as many of the native O'hia trees that had to be cut to make room for the structures at Yoga Oasis were then put into those buildings. As Sapphire showed me to the dorm-style room I'd be staying in and then around the grounds; I felt a connection I hadn't felt in a long time. Perhaps, the last time was years before when I had first visited Hawaii.

When My daughter was in the 6th grade, I had been invited by a client friend on a weeklong trip to Maui. I had been training this woman because she was due to have a major transplant surgery to alleviate her diabetes. Seeing how strong and healthy she'd been becoming under my tutoring and what a difference she'd felt, she had offered to take me on this trip expense free.

Despite spending the majority of days in the rain, we both had had a blast. We had rented a car and drove the entire way around the island. We had partied every night with cocktails and good food. We'd even met a couple of guys at a beach restaurant. They owned a catamaran and offered to take us whale watching and snorkeling for free. This trip had been wonderful and had left an impression on me as to what it might be like to live in Hawaii.

As Sapphire walked me around the facility at Yoga Oasis, I was introduced to other work/trade folks staying there. Some were in charge of building and grounds maintenance, others in room cleaning and laundry, and still another who, like me, prepped and served the food. Since I had a background in weight training, I was also going to help with a bit of fitness training. It seemed everyone who was here really wanted to be here but, more importantly, really believed in the ultimate mission of the place. With all-encompassing arms around it, Yoga Oasis had an authentic feeling of balance, of OM, to it.

Both Sapphire and the other cook trained me in the kitchen for a couple of days. I was in charge of brunch while the other cook had the evening meal. Brunch was a huge meal offered at 10 am to take the place of lunch for guests participating in Yoga Oasis retreats as well as those taking early yoga classes. The headcount varied between 20 and 30 people regularly.

My duties started quietly at 6 am. There had to be two kinds of tea freshly made and ready at 7 am for those taking the earliest yoga class. I had to prep the many fruits and vegetables collected from the grounds for massive fruit platters and salads, make whole grain breakfast muffins and porridge, and make the organic soy or almond milk from scratch. Poi (a starchy, but highly nutritious, savory pudding made from the taro root), fresh coconut, and raw honey had to be on the tables at all times. I needed to exit the kitchen by 8 am when the gong went off signifying the start of yoga. All was to be quiet.

I returned to the kitchen around 9:30 am to set out the food quietly. It was just like what you would see at a resort hotel except organic, made from scratch, and sourced locally first. Artfully arranged, were slices of banana, mango, pineapple, and oranges as well as the more exotic rollinia, abiu, sapote, jaboticaba and poha berries. Colorful veggie salads and sea greens complimented the homemade muffins and porridge. By 10 am, classes were ending, and I had to be finished.

Cleanup was also my responsibility. Though the mess was daunting at times, there was somebody around to help most days. Even so, I was usually done by noon. I did this six, sometimes, seven days a week. I got into the routine quickly and soon found myself in a satisfying and productive groove.

I Am Home

After the morning gong sounded, I would jump on my bike and ride to the ocean. I found a pretty state park on a bluff about six miles from the retreat. It was an easy ride down a very steep and narrow hill but a difficult ride back when I was in a hurry to set out brunch by 10 am. I had the afternoons to myself and explored as much of the Puna District as I could by foot or bicycle. Sometimes, I would hitchhike to the farther locations. In the first month alone, I saw all the top spots plus a few more extraordinary ones recommended by the locals.

Not surprisingly, I fell in love with the paradise around me. Every day, I saw the colors of the rainbow. From the green of the foliage and the different blues of ocean and sky to the beautiful array of colors of the fruits and vegetables I handled every day, I felt light and happy. Blessed.

The culture, style of life, and people also secured my love. So much different than living on the mainland, the aloha spirit was genuinely thick around these parts. A melting pot, Pahoa, and its surrounding communities welcomed anyone who carried no judgments. Young and old hippies and yogis are laid back, happy people who weren't caught up in what you wear or drive or do for a living. This place didn't keep up with the Joneses. Almost everything was accepted as long as you were not hurting anyone else, and most everyone tried to live as close to nature as they could. Clothing was optional at the beaches, and sustainability wasn't just a word. I was learning an entirely new way of life. It felt so right to me.

The raw and vegan crazes were hugely popular during this time. Because I was around such abundance of locally grown and organic ingredients, I took full advantage. The hour a day we were allowed on the computer at Yoga Oasis was first spent researching raw/vegan nutrition and new recipes. I began to lose weight though I didn't notice. The foods were good, toxin-free, and I felt so free-spirited.

I also spent some of my allotted web surfing time to join green singles and raw food singles sites. Not hoping for any serious relationship, I just wanted to meet other fun, active people on the Big Island, so I didn't have to experience all of these wonderful things alone. I became online friends with a few men, even met one at Volcanoes National Park and met a few more just by getting out.

As a newcomer to the Big Island, I was told by many that Pele might test me. Pele is one of the ancient gods of Hawaii. She resides in the magma pit of Halema'uma'u Crater on the side of Kilauea Volcano. Legends paint her as a fiery-tempered sister fleeing sibling rivalry and love 'gone wrong.' She can spill lava forth destroying everything in its path, yet has the compassion to save those who have not angered her. These tests she puts forth test the character of a person. Those who pass have her blessing and will live in bliss. Those that do not pass have her blessing to leave.

My first test came early. I was on my bike headed back up the steep and narrow hill just before Yoga Oasis. The sound of a large truck came up behind me, so I hugged the trees as close as I could. He clipped me quickly with the front of his bumper. Luckily, he stopped to see if I was okay, and I was. But as he drove off, he clipped me again with the boat trailer he was pulling. This time, it knocked me off my bike. The spill gave me some minor abrasions and bruises, and it bent my bike. I had to walk the last two miles uphill pushing my bike. Sapphire came running to help as I trudged up the driveway. She gave me the rest of the day off to recuperate. I healed. My bike was fixed. All was good in paradise again.

The second experience began down at Kehena Beach. Kehena is a black sand, clothing optional beach that is about 18 miles away from Yoga Oasis. On Sundays, there is a drum circle, fire twirling, and dancing. It's a place to let your cares and clothes go. I was laying down in the sand, after arriving, when an acquaintance from another retreat came and sat down. We talked easily, and then she asked if I wanted a dried mushroom. She knew I was a raw foodie, so I thought nothing of it and nodded yes. As she gave me one, she said, "Have a nice trip," and simply walked off. I soon found out being dried was not its only component!

I'd spent my life avoiding drugs. As a young teen, a friend had snuck one of her parent's cigarettes, and we tried it under cover of Devon Woods. She had puffed on it, enjoying every bit of it, while I tried it once and felt as if my lungs were going to get coughed out of my mouth. In high school, I had relinquished a marijuana joint to my father after finding it on my way home from school, and besides, I had always been too busy between school, home-work, and all of the extracurricular activities. College was wild, but I had preferred a little drinking and a lot of dancing. Even during my bodybuilding years, I had used natural supplements and stayed drug-free. A mushroom trip had never been on my agenda.

I became very disoriented and nauseated. I fell in the ocean and cut myself on the rocks. I tried to bike the 18 miles back to the Oasis, but my balance was off, and I noticed I had a flat tire. I couldn't ride with no air and no brain. I hitched a ride with a guy in a pickup truck who let me ride in the back with my bike. Though she helped herself to a laugh, Sapphire also helped me once I got back to Yoga Oasis. I was still dizzy and very weirded out. My body made it quite clear that I was not a drug user. I was also only 103 pounds of raw veganism and had no fat to absorb any toxins.

Despite these two unexpected adversities, I still embraced all that was Hawaii. Every aspect of this place felt better than any-where else I'd ever laid my head. The scenery, the people, the way of life just came so easily for me here. Sooner than I wanted it to be, my three months were up. I asked Sapphire if I could stay. Her response was frank and truthful. "No, Kieba. You are too good for this, and you should have your own retreat."

A flood of emotions roared through me: hurt that I could not continue on this same path, elation that she had that kind of confidence in me, disappointment in remembering I had a home to take care of in Kokomo, and pure energy to think that I could have a retreat of my own. My dream board exiting rehab had pictures of a tropical place where I was fit and healthy. Maybe, this was the natural extension to that - a place of my own to teach nutrition and exercise while having awesome adventures, in paradise, and hopefully, growing in both my personal and lifestyle realms.

My definition of Heaven, literally, had just expanded.

Grandma

I spent one more month in Hawaii before I returned to Indiana. During this time, I contacted a real estate agent friend of Sapphire's. I was barely in the car before she started smoking weed. We drove around for a bit as she hot-boxed her car, but it soon became obvious she had no time for me because I didn't have an unlimited budget. I found another real estate agent named John who bent over backward for me.

I wanted at least an acre of raw secluded land that was not more than five miles from the ocean or ten miles from town. Ideally, I wanted to go solar and live off the grid, but being a single woman, I also knew that having the convenience of county water and the availability of electricity was more realistic. Since I wanted to build a variety of structures such as a home, a cabin for my guests, a gym, and a climbing wall, I needed a subdivision that had less restrictive regulations. John showed me many places and continued to send me pictures after I left for Indiana.

Back in Kokomo, I felt like a different person. Having been a single mother for so long and helping my daughter take flight, the emptiness of any home I could make hit me harder than I expected. I also felt trapped and stagnant in the small-town Midwest where I had grown up and wanted to be closer to nature and the magical ocean. After spending four months in a paradise among like-minded, free-spirited people, that didn't want anything to do with the rat race so prolific in mainland USA, I knew I had found Hawaii to be a place I would call home.

Perhaps, most importantly, I no longer felt lost or without purpose. I loved my newly renovated house as well as my family, but the person I had grown into didn't have a place in Indiana anymore. The path for me, not as a mother, but as a woman living a dream, had been cleared and now needed to be groomed. As much as I wanted my daughter with me always, I knew it was time to let her live her life and find out how to live my own life.

Though other people noticed the changes and were supportive of my lifestyle changes, my grandmother was perhaps the most prominent motivator for me. We spent time together every day. She told me stories of her and Grandpa Blacklidge, back in the day, and we went on drives around Kokomo looking at trees and flowers. One day, as we were talking story, she tells me, "Honey, you need to be where your spirit soars free. Go back to Hawaii, and do not stay here for me or anyone."

Just as Sapphire's statement did, back in Hawaii, it hit me like a brick. With such simplicity, my grandmother summed up my predicament ever so neatly. Family had always meant so much to me, yet here I felt like I was stuffed in a can. I had spent so many years trying to be a decent provider, but now it didn't need to be my first priority. I could spend my time realizing my own potential. It was just what I needed to hear from the top matriarch in my life. Action came swiftly after that.

I listed my house in Kokomo for sale. I started to sell my possessions. John, the real estate agent, in Hawaii, continued to send me pictures of properties. As suddenly as things started making sense, it all screeched to a halt when I got a call from my dad, early one morning, about a week later.

He told me to sit down and then proceeded to tell me that Grandma Blacklidge had died. My dad's wife had gone to check on Grandma that morning, and after hearing no answer to her knock, she had found Grandma already gone. I crumbled to the floor, devastated, in disbelief and utterly heartbroken.

Just two days earlier, Grandma had been lucid, healthy and active during our afternoon together. She had asked me to stay a while longer. She said the house seemed so big without Grandpa. Weeks before, she had brought out all of her special possessions and told me the story behind each one and to whom she wanted each one to go. She'd done the same thing with Autumn before Autumn had gone to college. And now she was dead.

To compound the family's grief, no autopsy was ordered despite questions surrounding Grandma's death. Like the black cloud of doubt that surrounded the passing of Grandpa Blacklidge a few years earlier, we all wondered about the care and dignity Grandma had been given. I remember both my dad and his wife talking about Grandma during what ended up being her last days. None of their words were nice, and both had complained about how needy she was.

Many people came to honor the life of Marian Blacklidge. Family and friends came from all corners to offer condolences and share heartwarming stories. The town mourned the loss of such a dear woman. It was very uplifting to see how far the good hands of my Blacklidge name had traveled because my Grandpa and Grandma had been such true and genuine people.

During the days following my Grandmother's funeral, my grief was unshakeable. My dad tried to alleviate some of it by taking me to a psychic's fair outside of Indianapolis. He knew I liked the vibe on that sort of stuff, and I willingly went along because, through it all, I still wanted my father. There were about 25 psychics giving readings at the fair. My dad sat down at one of the first ones we saw, but I wanted to wait and see if there was a psychic I was drawn to meet.

He was an older gentleman with purple candles burning at his table. Before I could even sit down, he said there was a female entity with me who had recently passed. He went on to say that she wasn't gone yet, and she wanted me to know that she was okay and that she loved me. Tears flowed down my face unbidden. The psychic ended the reading by saying she will take the form of a butterfly, and be with me always. It was such a simple reading. The comfort I gained from it was so powerful. How he knew was indeed his gift, and the message he imparted helped me to heal in those tough times.

As is common among families that have a sudden death, squabbling over the family jewels, possessions and money began. In reality, though, there was no squabbling. It appeared to all of us that my dad's wife just took it. Within days of my Grandma's passing, she was driving my grandmother's car and wearing her jewelry. Soon after that, my dad and his wife moved into the Blacklidge house.

To me, stuff is just stuff. We all have our prized possessions or certain items intertwined with memories that we can't part with but, for the most part, we can get today what we lost yesterday. Though it was sad not to see Grandma Blacklidge's belongings into the hands of their rightful owners, it was more unsettling to see the entitlement my dad's wife took. Neither Grandpa nor Grandma had ever enjoyed the company of my dad's wife, but she had been accepted because she was the mate my dad had chosen. Now she was parading around Kokomo as "The" Mrs. Blacklidge, sleeping in my grandparents' bed and expecting the level of honor my grandparents had worked hard to attain. It had been hard enough to watch the slow detachment and degradation of my father, but this was just too much. I needed to get out of town and move on.

Within the month, John sent me information on a piece of property, and I bid on it. It was everything that I wanted. The undeveloped one-acre parcel of land turned out to be quite close to Yoga Oasis, so I was familiar with the street it was on. It was about five miles from Pahoa and four miles from the ocean, on a paved road and was complete with electricity and county water. The lot was agriculturally zoned, so there were no rules or regulations regarding what I could build, and I could have animals as well. The property had been willed to two sisters living in California who had never even been to the Big Island. I offered $25,000, and they accepted.

Suddenly, I had a piece of property in Hawaii! Before I could start taking reservations for my dream retreat, though, I needed to build, and I needed a place to live while I was building. I scoured Craigslist for possible caretaking positions in homes nearby. Within days, I found the perfect place. Three miles from my new property, a couple needed someone to take care of their home, pool, and property. They usually only visited about a month out of the year but would periodically have guests rent the main house. I would live out back in the pool house, clean the main house anytime there were guests, and maintain the pool and property. Despite only seeing a few pictures of the place, I committed to a one-year stay, knowing that it would take at least that to get something going on my property. The owners wanted me in by September 1st, so I had barely two months to sell, ship and prepare myself for one of the biggest leaps of faith in my life.

After a month, I had lightened my load substantially. I had sold all of my big furniture and my motorcycle. What I couldn't sell went into a storage place. That's when I realized a car sure would help when I got to the Big Island. Craigslist, again, provided. In an ironic twist, a couple living in Kona were moving back to Indiana just as I was leaving Indiana and coming to Hawaii. I bought their Geo Tracker. They even agreed to leave it at the Hilo airport for me.

It seemed as if my path was lined with light. Everything was falling into place easily, and I knew that this was exactly what I had to do. Right before I left, my dad had a little cookout for friends and family to come and say their goodbyes to me. Though it was sad to say goodbye, my heart felt strangely empty. I loved all of these people and had so many memories in this place, yet it seemed most of me was already somewhere else. I was just biding time, waiting for my life to really begin.

PART THREE

*Living Life With
Passion and Purpose*

The very place I'd been running from much of my life is now the place I am running to…back to myself…where true happiness and pure joy are found, and my full power switch is on.

Falling Into Place

*A*s an entrepreneur making a dream into reality, every step is a huge accomplishment, and there really isn't ever a grand opening. Nothing turned out as glamorous as when the dream first entered my mind, yet it's glamorous beyond measure because it's mine. A self-made business owner must have a single track mind but also be receptive to opportunities that lay off the road. And just because I said "self-made" doesn't mean that I didn't have help from a huge group of incredible friends, both new and old.

There were about three years between my departure from Kokomo armed only with a vision and a piece of property and the first official camper to my all-inclusive boot camp.

The first year was spent caretaking someone else's property as I built on mine. My knowledge of edible plants and tropical survival soared during this time. There were citrus trees of all kinds, avocados, chestnuts, coconuts, kumquats, starfruit, and chico sapote in the orchard I maintained. Collecting was fairly easy as I walked the property often. I found passion fruit, mango, and guava on my bike rides, and I learned how to dig for bamboo shoots and dive for sea greens. Just as the gatherers knew from before my time, the earth provides many things, but there was more work to be done after the collecting. Finding recipes and learning how to prepare all of the new fruits and veggies was difficult, but the entire process was exhilarating and felt so right.

Eating what I could, off the land, definitely required more of my time yet grounded me in many ways. Most of the plants I gathered were nutritional powerhouses, and I knew these skills would be awesome to incorporate into the meal planning of my boot camp. Knowing that I collected, processed, and prepared some of the food I ate helped me to actually live a life more sustainable for both our earth and my health. By spending less at the grocery store, I was able to spend more on my land. Life was not easy, but it was good.

As I ventured out to meet my neighbors and get to know my new hometown, the connections I needed to start things on my new land fell together easily. One of my immediate neighbors was kind enough to tell me he'd watch out for me seeing as how I was a lone woman living in a pool shed on a largely empty piece of property. He said I only needed to yell, in an emergency, and he'd hop the lava rock wall that separated us. He also had his own concrete business, so he'd be my foundation guy when I started on my house. Common in a small town, Sapphire, from Yoga Oasis, turned out to be friends with two people who offered services I needed. I met the plumber, almost immediately, while I was in town one day. Then, at the Sunday Maku'u Farmer's Market, I met the other who had a bobcat and cleared land. That same day, I met another man who knew a builder. Within a month, I was ready to begin.

Out of all the wonderful people who helped me push back the jungle and build a dream, there was a builder that stayed with me the longest. He made a lasting impression. His name was Marty, and meeting him was like seeing someone I had already known for years. He was a very thin, 50-year-old man, who looked older due to his white hair and long beard. He had soft, kind blue eyes and seemed very gentle. He told me what he'd built in the past and drove me to a few of the homes that were nearby.

He was a homeless man living out of his van with his dogs. He was brilliant, but he was also an alcoholic and smoked up to two packs of cigarettes a day. He offered to build my house in exchange for buying him all of the tools he needed and letting him live on the property until it was complete. I said I'd pitch in for food, but I drew the line at cigarettes and beer. We made a deal, and he was my guy.

The year in the pool shed went quickly but not without drama and adventure. I was out for a bike ride, about a month after I landed when my leg was bitten by a pit bull who got off his chain. That was my first of many encounters with Dr. Dan and the Pahoa Family Health Center.

The man who cleared my land would bring flowers and get well cards when I wasn't feeling well or after I hurt myself trying to help him which ended up being fairly often. He also brought home-grown marijuana, or pakalolo as many called it locally, which I preferred to the pharmaceutical pain-killers especially after the dog attack.

After I got all of my official papers stamped, signed, and filed, I got a cat from the local Humane Society. She was a fluffy tiger striped kitten who made me fall in love with her calm demeanor and big yellow eyes. I named her Malia, and she spent most of her time climbing the trees I maintained.

In October, the building began. The slab had been poured, the plumbing was set, County water came running out of the pipes, and the electric company put in a temporary pole so that I could draw power. Marty was putting up beams, within a month, when I had been told it would take me six months or more to wade through all the governmental red tape. I visited the property daily to help where I could. The heavy lifting was left to Marty and the helpers he had on any given day, but I nailed, carried, and lifted everything else I could. It was amazing how fast the base of the house went up, and it was very exciting for me.

Driving up to my property one day, I saw a puppy at the end of the drive. I got out and started calling to it. Suddenly, Marty was running headlong down the driveway, yelling at me that it wasn't a dog. Turns out it was a cute baby pig with a big momma nearby. I hopped back into my car really fast, laughing at how blonde I could sometimes be.

My mom bought all of her kids and grandkids plane tickets and arranged for us to stay at our own retreat in the Florida Keys in November. I had a great time with the whole family but felt very estranged from my daughter. It felt as if she was angry at me. I did not know why. Maybe, it was my weight because I was back down to 102 though I felt very healthy and was active out in nature rather than working out. Maybe, it was because I was 7000 miles away, and it was easier for her to talk to my sister who lived nearby. Whatever the reason, I felt distant from her during this trip. It made me miss her all the more.

I was sunning one day at a secluded pond when I saw a man that looked very familiar. When I had been back in Indiana getting ready to leave for Hawaii, I began looking at an online dating site called "Raw Singles." I searched for men who were already in Hawaii, and I was positive I was looking at one as I sat basking in the sun at Champagne Ponds. I called out his name, and I was right. Manis owned a retreat down the road from me called Pangaia and practiced what he called a "primal" all raw diet that included meats, dairy and eggs, absorbing Vitamin D from the sun, and maintaining fulfilling relationships. We became great friends and still are, but we have more of a brother/sister relationship rather than a sexual one.

I tried the online dating thing for a while again after seeing Manis. There were even a couple of men that I met through Match.com who flew over to meet me. Each time, I was treated with kindness, but there was never that spark that made me think of them as more than nice guys. I eventually became so frustrated I pulled my profile from the site. At this point, I felt I was just meant to live alone, and surprising even to me; I was okay with it. I was happy and living a dream.

In May, I became very ill with a high fever and wracking abdominal pains. Dr. Danny suspected leptospirosis which is a deadly bacteria acquired from drinking dirty water since I cooked and bathed from my catchment water. Thankfully, the tests came back negative for leptospirosis, but the results showed my liver stressed and my gallbladder area was very painful to the touch.

After listening to my dietary history, he concluded that my gallbladder was inflamed from some of the new fats I had been introducing into my diet here in Hawaii. I had to take some medicine and cut back on the rich fats like avocado, coconut, and macadamia nuts. In a week, I was better and incorporated a more modest intake of those offending fats.

I had been in Hawaii barely a year and thought I might die several times. Instead of tucking tail and running, I took all of them as tests on how to deal with extreme situations on my own. I wanted to be here. I wanted to spread my knowledge of nutrition and exercise. I wasn't going to quit. Pele' may have been playing tricks on me but to live inside the nets she flung was to live in the presence of spirits and the nature they commanded. Life was hard, but it was simple and good with a purpose always leading me true.

More Tests

The year in the pool shed left me just short of moving onto my property. All I needed was a couple of months, but I was unprepared to camp that long, and I couldn't afford a hotel room. Grasping at straws, I walked into a realtor's office and asked if anyone needed a caretaker immediately.

By luck of some kind, there was a house in need of a human presence. It was a brand new house with all the appliances but no furniture. It had water and electricity but no cell service nor land line. The owner wanted someone to stay there because thieves had stolen the hot water heater and water catchment already. I told myself it was only eight weeks.

Many nights in that house, I sat awake on my futon mattress in the middle of the empty living room floor with a flashlight and pepper spray. I worried the thieves would return. The neighbors fought all the time, and the police were called on a regular basis. They also had big, loud dogs that would come over anytime. After being bit by the dog on my bike, I was a little skittish around dogs. I told myself it was only eight weeks.

To rub salt into the already rocky situation, I couldn't have Malia kitty stay in the new house with me. In the days leading up to moving out of the pool shed and into the empty house, I had tried to familiarize Malia with our property. I fed her morning and night in the shell of our house, hoping she would stay. Within two days of moving her over to the new house, she was gone. I tried but to no avail to find her.

Nine weeks after I moved out of the pool shed, I moved onto my property, into my own house! It was only a small room in the lower part of my house, but it was livable. On my second night there, a faint sound woke me from a dead sleep. I've slept through louder sounds than what I heard that night, but this one snapped me awake, and I'm grateful I awoke. There at the sliding glass door was Malia!

Just fur and bones remained of Malia. There was a deep cut on her neck from what I believe was her leg getting caught in her collar and remaining there until it cut to the bone. I cut the collar off, applied a compress made with goldenseal, liquid silver, and other healing powders, and wrapped gauze loosely around her neck. I gave her food and water, and then she fell asleep on my bed with me.

It was a miracle she survived. She has never been the same happy, frisky, cuddly cat I fell in love with at the Humane Society, but even now at this writing, she lives. She never strays far from the lanai, is very guarded, and wants to eat any chance she gets, which I, of course, allow.

When Marty had first moved onto my property, he had two dogs. There was Puna, a lab, and Buddy, a pit bull. After Malia came back, I suspected that the dogs might have had a hand in scaring her off in the first place. Puna was gentle, but Buddy was a bit intense. Buddy snapped at me one day and broke the skin on my arm, so I asked Marty to keep him tied up beside his van. Shortly after that, I was walking back from picking a papaya behind the house when Buddy broke his tie and attacked me.

In a flash, he was on me, snarling and snapping. The weight and speed of the dog easily knocked me down, and he chomped onto the nearest piece of meat - my leg. He chewed on it like I was dinner and then started to drag me across the driveway. I was kicking at him and screaming when I fell onto my hip. I tried to crawl away, but the pain kept me still. My hip was the first thing that hurt, not my leg, but my hip was bruised and out of place from the fall.

Marty had been working up on the roof but saw the raucous. He ran down, grabbed Buddy, and started to shove the handle of his hammer down the dog's throat. I told him to stop. I didn't want him to kill the dog. Marty looked at me as I lay bleeding and twisted in my driveway, not understanding. I couldn't stand to be the cause of someone dying, couldn't deal with the visual and spiritual baggage that comes with death, and don't believe that taking a life solves anything ever. Even before I got home later that day, Marty arranged for Buddy to live with his friend who had a fenced yard.

I drove myself to the clinic and was rushed in to see Dr. Danny again. He cleaned me up and sent me to X-ray. My hip was twisted in the attack, but only bruises and scrapes were sustained. I had scrape marks embedded with rocks from my driveway in various places on my arm and leg. There was a bite on my arm that required stitches, and Dr. Danny sent me to an orthopedic surgeon for an MRI on my knee. The MRI revealed torn ligaments and a need for surgery.

After surgery, Marty picked me up with an arm full of flowers and a bag of peaches. He didn't have much else to give, but he had a heart and was willing to lend a hand whenever he could. He asked me where I needed to go and laughed when I told him to go to a Starbucks. For as clean and sustainable as I strive to eat, Starbucks coffee gives me wings when I feel like I'm returning from a trip to Hell. He even carried me in to get my special coffee.

The Vicodin wore off quickly. I took one more, once I was home, but hated how it made me feel. The pain was horrible, but I knew I'd rather suffer the pain than dope myself up with pharmaceutical drugs. An old surfer friend who reminded me of Rip Van Winkle came by the next day. He brought what he called the Puna Butter. He told me he'd made the concoction of marijuana and butter and that only a quarter teaspoon, at a time, was necessary.

The butter was amazing. Within three days, I was trying to pedal my stationary bike and doing mild leg extension exercises. At my first check-up with the doctor, he was surprised to see so much improvement in both the surgical area and my range of motion. I didn't want to have a stiff, inflexible knee, so I worked it. I pushed through the pain and soothed it after with a dose of the butter.

Seven months later, I made my second video audition for the reality television show, *Survivor*. I didn't make it on the show, but during the video clip, I hacked down a rack of bananas and carried it off, climbed trees, and swam in the ocean. I had gone from bum to bionic, in less than a year, when torn ligaments in the knee are known be problematic.

Goodbye, My Friend.
Hello Bootcamp.

By the time I had my knee surgery, I was living in a cozy space on the second floor of my house. I had a futon, a TV, a small refrigerator, and a gas burner for cooking. There were some wooden shelves for a limited amount of things, a countertop for the burner, and I had a toilet that worked. It seemed there were always improvements from the day before, but near the end of 2005, I started to notice Marty working less and resting more. He said he didn't feel well and had developed a terrible hacking cough.

At my request, Marty finally went to the doctor just before Christmas. He was full of cancer in both of his lungs and his liver, and it was spreading fast. I often visited while he was in the hospital, bringing him all kinds of goodies every time. He grew weak and lost his hair from the harsh chemo treatments, but I continued to visit because we had become so close. When I had tried the dating thing, he'd been the big brother I needed. He laughed at many of my naïve, blonde moments but never made fun of me and made sure to slip in a few hints for next time. He made a house materialize out of the jungle for me.

In April, he was released. Many of his family members came to Hawaii to help him back to California but also to see the life he had created here. Marty brought every one of them to my house to show them his last hurrah. He'd always called it his baby, and my house showed the heart and soul he put into it every day. Though it wasn't totally finished when he was diagnosed, the house maintains his style and spirit and is a living monument to the friendship we had. Marty passed away later that month.

I hired a man I met in town to finish the little work that still needed to be done on the house. At the same time, I was busy preparing a spot on my land for campers. In a clearing halfway between the road and my house, I set up an eight-person tent with a table, chair, and queen size air mattress. Outside, was a small porch with a lantern hanging from a tree to light the way. Nearby, was an outhouse and shower. I had scored a toilet in great condition from the recycle station at the dump. Marty had given me the shower stall he found from the same place. I cleaned both with bleach and set them up together with enough screen for a makeshift bathroom. It was a small and pretty rough space, but it was a start.

Of the two floors of my house, I lived in the upper level, and the lower level I made into a community use area. I screened it in and put in a utility sink where any campers and I would wash dishes and brush teeth. There was a large table, a gas burner, and a mini refrigerator. It wasn't even close to the set-up I dreamed of, but I was still headed in the right direction.

My first ever camper was a friend of mine from Indiana. We had worked together when I was the fitness director at the Sports Center in Kokomo, so his familiarity took away much of the usual tension that comes with starting something new. He also didn't want to commit to the full program I had set out for my fitness and nutrition boot camp, but it was a positive transitional step for both of us.

For the first few weeks, he made progress. He lost weight, eased back on some of his medications and said that he felt like a clean, new, healthy person. Then, we went into Waipio Valley for a strenuous hike, and the bartering started. It started on the trail as silly little quips like, "I'll buy you a shirt for a beer," but when we returned home, it continued as time spent in the bar. We eventually came to an agreement that he wasn't willing to make the lifestyle changes I was trying to help him with, and I wasn't going to let him continue on that path in my house.

By the time he left, I was much more aware of what my retreat needed. I hired a guy to build a 10'x12' cabin behind my main house for my campers. Some friends helped me clear, level, cinder, and carpet an area large enough for a 10'x20' carport so that it could be my first gym. The community use area, downstairs in my house, had been converted to living space, so I had three usable living spaces and an outdoor gym.

Just after the cabin was completed, I met a young traveler in town who was looking for a place to stay for a few weeks. He knew how to make websites, and I knew I needed a good one to gain momentum for my boot camp. I offered a free place to stay in exchange for his services, and he agreed.

In January of 2007, Body Temple Boot Camp was officially launched. I advertised it as a mainly raw, vegan fitness retreat where all meals, daily training sessions and island adventures were included. Yoga classes and massages were available but not included. I immediately started getting hits and inquiries. Soon after, my first official camper came. She was a young and very talented photographer from California, and we were both fired up.

I soon found that no script was needed as I talked simply about my loves of nutrition and fitness with her. We traveled around the island, hiking, biking, or swimming as we took in the beauty of Hawaii. She took many stunning photographs and gave them to me freely. The pictures show more than I could have ever hoped. They chronicle the beginning of a dream come to life. The handiwork is new but rough. The jungle hovers close, yet it is held back by a solid sense of purpose. The experience, as a whole, cemented my foundation at Body Temple Boot Camp, and at the same time, it gave me wings that allowed me to follow the passions in my life. I felt like I was on my way.

To Vegan, Or Not To Vegan

Since moving to Hawaii, I had adopted a mainly raw vegan diet. The amount of local produce that I could get made it easy, and I had been able to incorporate the fats that I had previously shunned, so I felt that I was doing well. Despite growth in my diet realm, I was starting to feel weak and frail.

In the fall of 2005, a raw, vegan woman with a retreat in Sedona had learned of me and my raw retreat/Bootcamp in the makings in Hawaii. She called me and asked if I would speak at her annual 3-day event called the *Raw Spirit Fest*. I was billed as a bodybuilder following a raw foods diet with a raw nutritional fitness boot camp, and I put everyone through a mini-workout right from their chair.

It was here that I met Viktoras Kulvinskas, one of the founders of the Hippocrates Institute for Health and the raw food movement. The founding Mother is Ann Wigmore. They have healed countless people of all sorts of life robbing illnesses with a raw, vegan diet. Their premise is based on a simple concept first voiced by Hippocrates, the father of modern medicine, nearly 2,500 years ago: "Let food be thy medicine and medicine be thy food."

During this time, I had also begun to wonder how a strictly a raw food diet could affect a person's overall health. Years before, in the midst of my hard exercise and unbalanced diet phase, I'd lost my menstrual cycle, and it still hadn't returned. I wondered if maintaining this diet was keeping me from having one. Viktoras told me that not having my period should be looked upon as a positive, healthy thing because it meant I was already clean and free of toxins. I gobbled up his words knowing he was considered a brilliant man. Incidentally, he was a top computer consultant in the U.S., at the time, when he went to see Ann Wigmore for the healing of his auto-immune disorder. Viktoras' computer services were coveted by institutions including Harvard, The Smithsonian, MIT, and The Apollo Project before he quit all to devote his life to promoting healing with a raw, vegan lifestyle.

In February of 2007, after watching me for many years, Manis (the man from raw singles and owner of Pangaia primal retreat) gave me a book called, *We Want to Live* by Aajonus Vonderplanitz. He said, "Read this, please. I do not want to lose another friend to raw veganism." The book introduces the notion of eating raw everything - even raw meat, eggs and dairy. It stresses the need to know the source of your ingredients and to make sure they are organic, from the wild, free range, grass or naturally fed animals. It is an extreme diet in every way but developed to rid the body of toxins and to restore diseased bodies to optimal health. The author seemed, to me, to be a nutritional Einstein who was brilliant to the extreme. Aajonus had overcome severe childhood autism and two bouts of cancer with his raw, primal diet. He lived with many different primitive cultures to observe and participate in their eating and healing through food habits.

After I read the book twice, I went down to Pangaia and slammed it on the countertop in front of Manis. I said in all seriousness possible, "I want to do this. I am ready." As a retreat, Pangaia was already promoting a raw, primal culture where most of the people living there adhere to living off the land. They maintained goats, caught local fish, grew many fruits and vegetables, and bought or traded for other free-range meat and raw honey.

Coincidentally, as I was grilling Manis for more information, one of the guests at Pangaia was a chef for the author of the book. He heard me asking questions and interrupted to ask me how long it had been since I'd eaten meat. When I told him it had been over 25 years for beef and pork, ten years for chicken, but I did occasionally have fish, especially within the last couple of years, he said we needed to start slowly. We would not want to throw my body into turmoil as I had when I incorporated the massive amounts of coconut, avocado, and macadamia nuts without prior introduction.

He went around the kitchen and gathered a spoon, the raw honey, and some raw dairy cream. He dipped the spoon into the honey, then into the cream and gave it to me. I barely slipped the spoon into my mouth, and I was in heaven. The silky fat of the cream mixed with the explosive taste of the raw honey burst open my senses, and I moaned. Though the chef recommended baby steps, he welcomed me to look into the two big refrigerators at Pangaia. One was full of fresh produce. From bottom to top, it was packed with vegetables and fruits. As I moved to the other fridge, I passed free range eggs and was told that eggs should not be refrigerated and were best if left on the counter for two weeks. I opened the door of the second fridge, and it was stacked with all kinds of meats and dairy. From liver to breasts and goats milk to cheese, it was all fresh and all raw.

On autopilot, I just let myself soak it all in. My eyes gravitated to a bowl of raw liver. My instincts kicked in, and before even thinking about it, I grabbed the dripping liver and started to devour it. Blood was dripping everywhere, and both Manis and the chef stood back in amazement. Immediately, my brain felt like it kicked into gear. An unexpected energy also came, and within hours of my raw snack, I could swear I became more grounded.

After years of feeling a bit airy and spacey, this primal way of eating changed my whole demeanor in just a few days. A calm descended upon me that I'd never been able to feel before, and I was able to focus more intensely on conversations. In three short months, I was so amazed by the results that I wanted to meet the author and hear him speak. I set out to organize a workshop in Hawaii with Aajonus as the keynote speaker.

I continued to eat according to this new raw everything diet as I was gathering other speakers and making arrangements for the Primal Diet Workshop. My research led me to an amazing company that sells free range and organic meats of all kinds. US Wellness offers a bountiful selection that includes many organ meats from different animals. All animals are raised in their natural environment and allowed to roam, graze, and play. I even spoke with the owner of the company, so I could tell him my story and hear more about his mission statement. As we talked, he said he had heard of Aajonus and was interested in meeting him as well as getting a consultation from him, so he agreed to become a part of the Primal Diet Workshop.

As the time of the workshop neared, my own body had improved from this diet. I had gained over ten pounds from all of the raw meats, dairy, and eggs. I still ate fruit, sparingly, due to the amount of sugar involved but compensated by eating loads of veggies. For the first time in years, the lab results from my doctor's appointments were perfect. I was very much looking forward to meeting this miracle man and spending time picking his brain.

Primal Raw To Retro Raw

*A*ajonus Vonderplanitz and the owner of US Wellness, John Wood, arrived in Hawaii at the end of April 2007. I drove to their accommodations every morning to pick them up. Sometimes, we would swim. Other times, we would relax. I knew I was in the presence of two brilliant men. I wanted to get to know the real men behind the professional faces they wore. The opportunity was a blessing to me. I was going to relish it.

The day of the workshop was buzzing. The room was packed, and it seemed that every person had a pen and paper scratching frantically as they tried to write down every word. It was a long eight hour day, but the amount of information covered was immense. John Wood came to me afterward, saying, "Aajonus is way out there, but he is absolutely correct in everything he said. He is brilliant."

After the speeches were done, Aajonus was available for consultations. These consultations were based on our answers from a lengthy health questionnaire drawn up by him as well as the results of an iridology reading. Iridology is the practice of looking at your eyes, specifically your irises, and gaining results from the different zones therein.

As I sat down with Aajonus, I was still in awe. The people I'd been able to bring together and meet during this workshop had all been amazing. I believed in this diet, though it had only been three months that I'd been dipping my fingers into it. I felt on top of the world, and this was my time to sit and talk with the Commander.

He told me to gain another ten pounds on top of the ten I had already gained the three months I'd been on the diet. He taught me that fat is what helps me to rid my body of toxins, so having some is better than having none. He pointed out where the greatest toxicities lay in my body and where I was weak, but he also congratulated me on graduating away from the harmful raw, vegan diet. I guess I wasn't as bad as some of the people he'd seen.

Aajonus gave me a diet plan to follow for the next three months that would target specific areas and provide me with the tools to accomplish what he pointed out to me in his consultation. I was already following much of it, so I just needed to pull a bit more together. With US Wellness, I was able to get the best quality meats through the mail. Aajonus had recommended that I eat organ meats, specifically, two to three times per week to help enrich my blood. Living on an island, fresh fish was available regularly and that provided healthy fats packed in lean protein. A neighbor had some hives and chickens. I easily was able to get the raw honey and eggs on a morning walk, bike, or run. Scouring the island for other ingredients, I found some farmers, about an hour away, who had cows and sold raw milk, cream, kefir, yogurt, and cheese.

I remember these months vividly. I felt so alive. I continued to train. I gained weight, and I knew I was eating the best food I could find. By the end of the three months, I was 112 pounds, and it was healthy muscle with a little fat to pad the edges. I loved it, but this was the most extreme diet I had ever followed. Without growing or raising most of the food I needed, the ingredients alone made the diet too costly to continue. After I regained my health, I also felt that it was too heavy on proteins and fats for a regular, permanent, lifestyle diet.

Over the next few months, I began to devise a new diet that would take the best of all the diets I'd tried throughout my life and marry them together. From my bodybuilding days, I knew that a low sugar, low grain, and low carbohydrate diet would promote lean muscles. As a raw vegan, for the last few years, I knew the nutritional qualities of eating raw couldn't be passed up. Adding the raw dairy and meats of the primal diet would ensure that the necessary proteins and fats were included. The new diet would be about 75% raw with light cooking *only* needed for the heartier vegetables and the super grains. I was trying to turn back the clock with this new diet, back to a time when humans ate mostly raw, whole foods and hunted, gathered, or raised most of what they needed. I called it the Retro Raw Diet.

As a culmination of my new creation, I gathered and created many raw recipes, illustrated them with help from my computer, and put it all in four different Retro Raw Recipes for Life books. I sent out the first bundle of books to John of US Wellness who sold them through his website. The local health food stores also picked up some copies, and I offered them for sale through my Body Temple Boot Camp website. Feedback was positive, and the whole concept was drawing some attention.

I saw this new diet as 'doable' for everyone - not completely raw, and not outrageously expensive, but nutritionally sound using ingredients familiar to most people and packed with flavor, too. John also saw the potential and invited me to help him in New York at the Health and Wellness Expo. That trip was exciting because I met Carol Alt and Kat James. Carol Alt, best known for being a supermodel, was speaking at the Expo about her once failing health and how following a raw diet that included meats and dairy helped get her back on track. Author of *The Truth about Beauty*, Kat James, was also there, and I was able to do a radio show with her.

I also incorporated the Retro Raw diet into my boot camp. I felt that the components needed for an incredible retreat were all coming together. With my first few campers, I figured out that daily activity could mean anything from hikes around the island to a hard-core workout session in my outdoor gym. The optimal nutrition part was getting re-worked, and I was very confident with my first-hand results. The combined efforts of fitness and nutrition will start anyone on the right path, but the addition of fresh air and sun could also reduce the amount of stress most people carried. In short, I was trying to create the perfect recipe for a vibrant, healthy, long life. The healing waters of the ocean were the icing on the cake, but I knew I was missing one integral aspect of my program.

All of the elements above could combine to make anybody healthy, but to adjust a person's mind to make their dreams come true was something I didn't know how to teach. This part is essential for complete healing of a person. From a young age, I knew I had it, but to help another person realize their own power of manifestation was out of my reach. To weave mind, body, and actions together and seemingly manipulate time and space may seem magical, too far out there, or unattainable, but it wouldn't be the first time somebody called me crazy. I knew that forming a mindset in line with fitness, nutrition, and a place of safety could be the base that could build *anything*.

The Campers

Campers trickled through steadily as the years passed. As varied as my first two campers were, my friend from Kokomo and the photographer who gave me pictures, every subsequent person came and left with their own stories. Each person had their own transformation, and I feel lucky to have been a part of each one.

Women have been the majority of my campers, but that doesn't discredit the men who've come. Most of the campers were single, though others came as couples or families; some traveled from as close as mainland America, but others came from India, England, Africa, and Japan. I've even been lucky enough to have several campers return for another stay. Every camper's story could be a chapter on its own, and I feel it's a travesty to generalize them all into one chapter, but I must make progress on my own story.

About the time I was making plans for the Primal Raw Workshop, I had a psychic stay with me. She was one of the top psychics in the world, but since she wanted to focus on her health and fitness, she refused to use her energy for psychic readings during her stay. Her stay was five weeks long, and she made great strides while she was here. Weight sloughed off as her diet improved, her daily exercise ramped up, and she remained positive throughout.

She was a Midwesterner, so we had much in common though it was plain to see I'd moved on from that lifestyle and culture. The conservativeness of her environment made her a bit uncomfortable when confronted with the clothing optional beaches, but she had a fantastic attitude, and her desire and drive to succeed overpowered any hesitation or judgment she may have harbored. Many times during her stay, we ended up laughing so hard we cried.

Though she put her energy into learning new habits, there were two times her psychic abilities couldn't be denied. One day early in her stay, and right in the middle of a workout, she asked suddenly, "Kieba, do you know someone named Jezebel who has passed on?" I didn't recognize the name but called my dad to see if he remembered anyone by that name. At first, the name didn't mean anything to him either, but suddenly, he remembered his Uncle Duke. He explained that my great-uncle Duke had been a powerful attorney in town and had had a secretary who was a force to be reckoned with in her own right. My dad said she'd adored me, and her name was Jessie Bell. This woman, my psychic camper told me, was one of my Spirit Guides and was with me at that moment.

Another time, when we were picking up raw milk from a goat farm, the owner was lamenting over a hurt baby goat. The little billy was only a day old, but he had gotten tangled within a barbed wire fence, and the owner didn't think he was going to make it. We peered into the box at the bloody kid. It immediately took me back to my days of Dawn's Infirmary, and I knew or somehow I felt this little goat was going to live. I picked him up, with his gangly legs and bloody face, looked him in the eyes and I told him, "By the power invested in me, you shall live and be fine. Now stand up." When I put him back in the box, the little billy stood up and bleated.

After the goat farm, we went to Pangaia to see Manis and meet a dear friend of his who was visiting. The friend was tall and very thin, and I felt that he wasn't well probably due to his raw, vegan diet. When I went to hug him, I felt such compassion for him and his journey because it hadn't been that long ago when I was in the same shoes. The psychic took a picture of me hugging him.

Within a week, the owner of the goats called me up and said the billy goat was doing fine and being bottle fed. She was astounded, but my psychic camper told me what she already knew. As I had picked up the kid and held him in my arms, she'd seen an aural light of purple coming from my hand. When I hugged Manis' friend, she said the purple light had remained. The photo of our hug was developed, and the light was there, too, emanating from my hand just as she'd told me.

To the unbelievers, there are a dozen explanations to define a mysterious light. I may even be a bit skeptical, yet as she left, one of the top psychics in the world, said that she'd never been in the presence of someone who held so much power of manifestation. She'd lived with me, watched me for over a month, and knew that if anyone wanted something and was able to see it as possible, it was me. In this way, I was able to make things happen. Whatever I wanted, if I knew it could happen, it would be true and real without a doubt. Somehow, this power of manifestation, of mindset, is what I wanted to communicate to my campers – 'a live as if' mentality.

Every camper came with hurdles. On the whole, it was the men who had the hardest obstacle to overcome - their own maleness. Their masculinity made them fun to coach, teach, and take on adventures, but they were also the most challenging with the most fierce habits, beliefs, and opinions. One insisted on putting chew in his mouth and watching football every Sunday while others thought they could sneak down the road to the hot dog cart or 7-11 for Big Gulps. Being a small town, I usually busted the sneaky ones, by chance running into them, or having my friends rat them out. The determination on my part to find the ways to break the worst habits or find the balance drives the point home for others.

As campers came and went, I integrated everything I could. I took note of what worked and what didn't work with what personality type. I was always researching fitness and nutrition and tweaking the program. I built an official Jungle Gym which was a major improvement over the 10'x20' carport gym. With an actual roof and screen to keep the bugs at bay, the gym also had a climbing wall on the outside of the tallest wall. This made camp an even better destination.

The 2008 Olympics were also a big idea maker. I watched the 42-year-old Dara Torres beat most of the younger girls, and she inspired me to become a better swimmer. I began lap swimming and practicing dives at the public pool in Pahoa. A friend of Manis' began to organize a small-scale Olympics for athletes who followed a raw diet. Called the Raw Games, athletes who wanted to enter had to be eating a diet at least 75% raw though they did not have to be vegan. I joined the committee, as an athlete, and was put in charge of the triathlon and the obstacle course.

As with the other events that were put together by all of the health and wellness leaders in Puna, the Raw Games were a huge success. The venue was the spectacular Kalani Resort which opened its 25 acres of lush oceanfront to organizers and athletes alike. Aajonus Vonderplanitz came again as well as Vegan Raw Guru David Wolfe. I had a camper at the time who was considered to be the Raw Primal Diet advocate of Australia. While men and women competed and the dietary visionaries spoke at workshops, I put all of my own diet knowledge together and fed a great many of them. Again, dipping into my contacts from the Raw Primal diet, I gathered raw honey and eggs from my neighbor, fresh fish from mere miles away, the great quality meats from US Wellness, and the raw dairy from the Farmers.

The overall feedback from the Games was fantastic. I learned of a few converts, locally, who graduated from raw veganism to a more raw primal diet. The emails I received from people thanking me for speaking about my experiences with both diets were amazing. Being able to spare even one person the downward spiral of following a clean but unhealthy diet pushes me to continue this work. Having met Aajonus and seeing firsthand how powerful he is, in his mature age, makes me strive to be better myself. Being a part of workshops and events that literally can save people, is what keeps me going.

Amidst all the planning and happenings of the Raw Games, my mom was planning her 70th birthday party. It was going to be a big event at the Kokomo Country Club, and over 100 people were invited. I thought I'd stay a month, maybe more, with the majority of it at my Dad's house and the rest at my brother's lake house.

Days before I was to leave, I got a call from my dad saying I couldn't stay at his house anymore. Hurt and confused, I tried to ask why and where else I was supposed to go and was his wife really behind this sudden change, but there was no more. My dad was unwilling to say more and unyielding in his stance.

Abruptly, I shortened my stay. I had tried to make peace with my dad's wife when I'd bought the house across the alley from theirs, but this wielding of my dad to do her bidding was too much. I'd seen it before and liked it less now that I'd been living peacefully and quietly in the jungle for so many years. Her drama was too chaotic for me to handle. I stayed in a hotel in town for a bit and then went to the lake house my brother offered me.

My mother's party was a huge hit. Seeing so many family members in a short amount of time was great though demanding. As we were all catching up inside, someone noticed my dad's wife outside. She was taking laps on a bike in the parking lot, looking up at the windows. Everyone started laughing. Comments like, "socially inept" and "can't lighten up and let loose" began to fly. My dad was nowhere to be found, and I didn't know whether to join the laughing or start crying.

When I did finally see my dad, he'd had to sneak around his wife to see me. At the time, he was working at the appraisal company he and my brother owned, so I just rode around with him as he conducted the reviews. I know my dad felt horrible, but he had nothing to say when I told him his wife was ruining his life. We sat in his truck and cried. I missed him so much. He'd always been my emergency call. I hadn't been able to count on him for years. I felt like I was losing someone I didn't want to lose. Worse yet, I wondered, on the long plane ride home, if I'd ever get to sit down with my dad without crying.

Relationships And Hope

I settled back into my Hawaii life gratefully. I didn't have boot campers all the time, but there was plenty enough social life around to keep me happy and never lonely. Whether it was the pool or the ocean, the café or an adventure, it seemed a friend was never far. Though I ultimately wanted to share this life with another; I was satisfied enough to stay single for now.

A friend went through a bad breakup, and when she asked me to dinner, in exchange for my help starting an online dating profile, I agreed. On the one hand, I was reluctant because the online dating thing just hadn't panned out for me, and I didn't want her to get her hopes up. On the other hand, this was an easy step to get her out there and move on from her ex of 18 years. We took a couple of "hot" pictures of her and made profiles on both Match. com and e-harmony. It was a fun night of goofing around with a friend, sharing a delightful dinner, and lifting each other ever higher as we sang about the magnanimous attributes we both had.

Lo and behold, in less than two months she was dating a man who lived right here on the Big Island, and within nine months, they married. I was ecstatic for her and began thinking maybe it was time for me, too. My last steady boyfriend had been the gallant 'Peaceful Warrior' whom I had dated before going to rehab. Rehab was in 2002, and it was now 2010. Before that, it was a string of liars and control freaks, two marriages that lasted barely a year each and an abusive relationship that ended in an abortion. I didn't have a good track record.

I reactivated an old profile on Match.com and uploaded a few new photos. I checked it too much and didn't find enough, so frustration started to set in. Reaching out to all the realms, I booked a session with a girlfriend of mine who was a Reiki healer and spiritual counselor. As I laid on my back with my eyes closed, I heard chimes and felt movements around my head I knew couldn't be her. When a jolt of energy rushed through me, I had to peek. She was down by my feet and said the energy was strong because I was very open and receptive.

We talked about the experience afterward, and she helped me find ways to focus my energy on love. There were mantras and other positive feeling exercises looking both inward and outward that would hopefully allow me to find a soulmate. Even after so many bad relationships, I still believed in the ideal.

Maybe that had started with my dad. For so long, it seemed that my parents had such a perfect life. We were a family unit, we did things together, we were always so close, and I thought my dad was at the head of it all. Even when he started questioning his own life choices and searching for other answers, I admired the vulnerability and honesty he showed. By the time my dad had begun drifting away, I was thoroughly ensconced in teenage self-awareness and had found 'love' with my upperclassman football quarterback.

If I would have kept that one, things may have turned out differently. Instead, I dumped him, so I didn't have to deal with a long-distance relationship and started down a path of less than stellar relationships. When I had stitched myself back together from the forced loss of a baby, and suddenly, the Don Juan of Kokomo was picking me out of all the other women he could've had, I thought I'd found him. Tall, lean, handsome and very funny, I saw myself living forever with him. I loved that he didn't take life too seriously, and I pictured a happy little family with a few children somewhere along the way.

When his eyes strayed, and random girls sat on his lap, I still wanted everything to be perfect. I believed so deeply in sharing Life with a man who I loved that I knew I could still make it happen. It took a year of not owning what my friends were saying, though somehow, I 'read' my friends, just not the words they said. When my heart finally understood, and I couldn't trust him any longer, the image of him as my soulmate broke.

My second marriage was pretty much doomed before our vows were said, but the blessing bestowed on me was the most powerful gift of love. The relationship was fun because it was the rebound after my marriage, and we both loved being involved in college frat life. It was just as we realized we weren't the most compatible that I found out I was pregnant. We tried to live the happy family life, but neither of us was happy. Husband and wife broke up, but the undeniable bond of mother and daughter remained. I had an endless pool of love for my daughter, and I had another one reserved for the man of my dreams. Only I couldn't find one worthy of my reflection.

The rest of my relationships were woven in with my body-building days and dietary craziness. None of them lasted long. Mental and emotional abuse, control issues, lies, betrayal and even theft, were my misfortunes, but I experienced them all and still knew I would look for that love so deep because I refused to be bitter. Building my dream allowed me to believe in myself again, made me see that a woman with a will already has the way, and I didn't need a man to be happy.

Being single for the last ten years had been great, but underneath it all, I craved that two peas in a pod, the balance of yin and yang, two parts of a whole conclusion. I wanted an adventurous and lighthearted soul who would run parallel lifelines with me until we fell down laughing and then roll, intertwining everything we had.

On August 7th, 2010, I was checking out some profiles on Match.com, and one stood out. The profile picture was of a bald head with goggle wearing eyes emerging out of the water like a crocodile. His other pictures chronicled some heavy duty adventures: climbing Mt. Kilimanjaro, swimming for ten hours straight for charity, riding his bicycle from Colorado to Canada and back on a dare, participating in the longest and hardest canoe race in the world. The demeanor in the man's pictures showed him to be serious and intense, verging on intimidating, and his physique was stunning. His blue eyes were noticeable in all the pictures, and though his muscles were like bricks, he was neither stout nor like Arnold. He wasn't the type of man who usually caught my eye, but as I read his words, I began to hope.

Seth Stanley stepped quickly into the arena. He said he hoped whoever reads his profile has already read many bios and been on many dates but still hasn't found someone who is perfect. His language was flowing and sensual but to the point. If I was the one for him, I needed to be gorgeous inside and outside, look great in jeans and stunning in a dress, humble but intelligent, honorable and enthusiastic and on and on. The list was lofty but attainable, and I recognized the majority as traits I actually had.

I was kind of giddy as I read his ideal woman's attributes. His words were moving, and I wondered if I could be the one he described as his ideal companion. As he started to describe himself, I got the chills. He spoke of being like a coach to those around him, what a great partner he is, and how he loves being challenged intellectually. Since he grew up in a mountainous state, the outdoors were an essential pleasure to him. He had a son, but I loved that he said, "he comes free inside the package if we're a match."

It was a long profile but not long-winded. He could have inflated everything, but even at half what he claimed, I was still impressed. His casual language seemed to read my mind, but it was clear enough to let me know he meant business. Seth claimed he'd spent a lot of time writing the words because he wanted to get to the good stuff faster. This wasn't my first time around the online dating thing, and I absolutely wanted to skip all the awkward wasted time on men who wouldn't deliver. I put him in my box of Favorites.

Dream Come True Or Just My Illusion

*T*o my unbelieving delight, I had a message from him in my box the very next day. Seth's profile had said he'd only wanted to date women who were in his area, and I was half-way across the country, but he'd written anyway. I could barely breathe. The air where I was seemed to be so thin. As I began to read his response, I laughed. It read like a questionnaire.

He was in one state, me in another, could it even work? He had a son. Could he actually try the dual state living, and why would I when I have established myself in Hawaii? But how could he set aside exploring a serious relationship after my profile rang so true to him? He closed by asking me what I thought, and what I had seen in his profile that sparked my eye. The light giggle that escaped me answered for me.

I was on popcorn strings. It was like the first time again, back in high school, hoping to impress, but so innocent, I could only be me. I was in awe but aware of my boundaries. There was no way I could ever move permanently back to the mainland, but I might entertain the thought of two separate worlds *if* he was the one.

For years, I had been driven to find a life mate. I strongly believed that he, too, was trying to find me. With the power in myself that I was beginning to realize and share with the world, I started to entertain the thought of a complementary power emanating from him. I messaged Seth back, saying that we have too much to offer and share, not only with one another but to the world. My communication was still somewhat relaxed, but my desire was hard to control. I constantly had to reel myself back in.

We began to communicate via email, and it quickly escalated to multiple emails in a day, calls, and even texts. Both of us were smitten. The depth of questions ranged from deep truths about our past relationships to silly side notes like which way do you put the toilet paper on the roll. Within a month, he decided to fly to Hawaii.

On September 3rd, 2010, Seth was on his way to see me for two weeks! Feeling like a teen again, I bought a sassy mini skirt and halter top at the local surf shop. We had agreed that I would fly from the Big Island to O'ahu and meet him at the Honolulu airport. On the plane, I had a drink to calm my nerves. I sat back and thought positive, loving thoughts, but none of it worked. I was a lump of nervous energy.

We were to land within ten minutes of each other. The mainland terminal is different from the inter-island terminal, so we talked to one another as we made our way towards each other. I asked what he was wearing, and just as I turned the corner, I saw him coming. My heart raced with excitement and anxiousness. Adrenaline began pumping through my stomach as if I were going into fight or flight mode.

Without any control or thought, I started to run towards him. Like a movie, we dropped our bags and ran, arms wide until

I almost bowled him over. It was non-stop sputter and disbelief through the airport - is it really you? Are you really him?

We went to a hotel not far from the airport and got one room. ONE ROOM! We unloaded our bags and headed straight to the rooftop for drinks, music, and talking. Talking live, face to face. I was still nervous as hell about having this man with me for the next two weeks. I had not shared my life with any man, on a daily basis, for many, many years, but I was amazed. Astounded and daring to dream, my smile could not have been erased that night.

I had not been intimate for quite some time, but being with Seth was a breath of invigorating fresh air. Everything had just come so easily, slid into place and felt incredible. He proved to be a gentle, patient, romantic and passionate man. He seemed perfect. I wanted him to be perfect.

For two weeks, we lived in the moment. I was blissed out and loving every minute. We played tourist, and I showed him every place I could think to show him. We shared and connected on many levels, and I loved that he gave professional attention to my swimming. I knew it was the love and lust stage of a new relation-ship. As much as I craved the contact, I'd also had so many hurtful experiences that I couldn't help but hear the little voice that said, "Be careful, this may be too good to be true."

I stuffed that voice deep and agreed to visit his hometown. Before he left, Seth bought a one-way ticket for me that was dated for the following month. I could buy the return flight whenever I needed to. I thought that was fair.

Seth left. I was left to think way too much of him. We talked or texted often. I went about my business, but everything I did had an undercurrent of Seth. I tried not to be head over heels, but my desires were already a step ahead of me.

I decided to perform a little ritualistic ceremony, partly to acknowledge him in my life and partly to create space. I wrote a love letter to him, rolled it up, and stuffed it into a pretty blue bottle. I corked it and tied a simple twine bow. I planned to take it to Mackenzie Park and toss it far into the ocean in hopes that someone would find it somewhere and send it to him. Yes, I had included his address.

Before I headed to Mackenzie, I stopped by the café for a cold-pressed espresso coffee. I didn't have them often because of the caffeine, but this was an occasion that I felt called for it. After most of my drink had gone, and I was done socializing, I took off for the park. The drive and the mission were both refreshing. I knew if I could find the balance necessary for both of us, this was going to be the relationship of a lifetime. The sun filtering through the coastal trees canopied over the road and made for a magical environment meant for such an occasion.

I arrived at the park and saw a friend immediately. He was just relaxing, finding some peace away from his busy life, and drawing out the moment with a joint. In a place where marijuana is so prolific and accepted, it was an offer from a friend I took without question. I was at this gorgeous, sacred place to perform a special act so, I took a hit, thanked him and then headed on my way, armed with my blue bottle.

I didn't even make it halfway to where I had envisioned before the world started spinning. The combined effect of the coffee and the pot hit me like a nuclear bomb. I immediately turned around and used every ounce of focus I had to get myself back to my car. It was only four miles to my house, but once on the road, I knew I wouldn't be able to make it. I was losing consciousness; my heart was beating out of my chest, even breathing became a chore. I pulled into a friend's driveway but couldn't get out the door, so I just laid on the horn.

My friend came out and helped me into her home. I collapsed on the couch and just tried to concentrate on breathing and staying calm. It felt like I was drowning, like the last bits of oxygen were becoming water, and I needed to adapt but couldn't. I wanted to go to the hospital, but no words came. I lost consciousness.

My grandfather appeared. He starts talking and says, "Junior Jerk." I knew right then I had to get it together. My grandfather tells me he sent Seth for a reason, and I had better get my head straight. I then reach out to Seth. In a way, that is only possible in the darkness, I tell Seth that I need help getting out of this. I was giving him the toughest coaching job of his life, in both love and long distance, and that he'd better help me or I wasn't going to make it. And then I slept.

My friend was there when I woke up about an hour later. She gave me some tea to drink and some raw honey and cream to coat my stomach. I slept for another hour. When I woke again, I finally felt stable enough to be driven home. Safely back at home, tired but conscious, I checked my phone.

There were no less than 15 missed calls from Seth and texts that started, "Where are you?" and grew quickly to "Call me back!!" I texted a short note and told him I'd fill him in tomorrow, but sleep was supreme. In the morning, I was still buzzing but could function. I explained the whole thing to Seth, and he sternly asked me never to smoke weed without him again.

I wanted to roll my eyes and told him I thought that was a little ridiculous. We argued about it. I didn't like being told when I could or could not do something, especially since I lived in a place where the majority of the population partook in the mood-altering plant. In the end, I was struck by how much he cared and showed genuine concern for me, so I yielded. It was a small request for his regard for my safety, so I thought.

Charm And Red Flags

On October 15th, 2010, I put my house and kitty in the loving care of a friend from the coffee shop and embarked on a journey that held both joy and anxiety. I was headed to a strange place to stay with a strange man and his son for an undetermined amount of time, but for the first time in a long time, I was experiencing a love that I'd always longed to have in my life. Texas would not have been my first choice of states to live, but I'd heard lots of great things about Austin, so I was keeping an open mind. I also wanted to see his life on his turf.

He met me at the airport with open arms. There were flowers and a bottle of wine waiting in a huge truck. Then, he took me to the largest Whole Foods I'd ever seen. When we pulled up to his enormous house just outside the city, a rock settled in my stomach. I wondered if he thought me a pauper in my jungle home compared to this palatial estate that housed one and only occasionally two people. His dating profile had mentioned he was in the $500K and up income category, but until this point, he had given me no outrageous indication otherwise.

Though I felt like a fish out of water as I fingered the marble countertops, Seth had gone beyond regular care to make sure I felt comfortable. From our time together in Hawaii, he had an idea of what I liked to eat, and then he also asked me before I arrived if there were any items he could get. I knew things would be stocked, but I didn't expect four of everything I'd requested. The refrigerator was so full I wondered if we'd be able to eat it all before it spoiled. I had to chuckle.

On the second morning in Austin, I met Seth's ex-wife and his 14-year-old son. Conversation with his ex-wife was brief but easy and meeting his son brought back many memories. Seth's son, Ben, was very polite and full of manners, but I recognized some mannerisms and behaviors from my past work with autistic children in Indiana.

I was more than a little anxious our first morning together and overthought everything. I didn't know if I should make breakfast and if they'd like what I made or if they had a usual morning routine. The rock in my stomach rolled around as silence became the majority conversation holder at the table. Breakfast had always been light or loud or silly in my house, and this serious atmosphere was jilting. I felt I needed to sit and be quiet, so the rock kept rumbling.

This was not the last anxious moment I'd have in Austin. Most of them I was able to brush off, but I began to realize that if it had been any other relationship, I would have been quick to end it. If we had lived in the same town, I would have just left and gone back to my happy-go-lucky lifestyle, but for some reason, I felt a pull that told me to hang in there. After all the years without a relationship and finally finding a man that I had so much in common with, was not something I could just flippantly toss aside.

Real-time life with Seth was busy. There was a lot of commuting since his son went to a private school in Austin. Seth was also in the middle of downsizing since his trek up Mt. Kilimanjaro had left him humbled and with a feeling that he needed to simplify. I found out that Seth rented the huge house which was a relief, yet I still wondered why he'd picked such a gigantic rental when he lived alone most of the time. We began posting items on Craigslist. My tentative two-week stay got longer.

I had been in Austin about a month when I called Jon Fox, aka Hilarion, one of the top psychics in the world. I was having difficulty balancing the conflicting feelings of love and anxiety I'd been having in this relationship and wanted to see if I could gain any insights. I was informed that this was the seventh lifetime together for Seth and me, and it was in this lifetime that we must work together to reach as many people as we could with our powerful combined message. Hilarion said there would be challenges, but I shouldn't take flight. He confirmed that my grandfather did have a part in sending Seth and that it was all for a higher purpose. That purpose would be clear in time.

Soon after that, Seth approached me about borrowing money. He reluctantly told me about some poor financial decisions and said he fully expected his income to increase in the new year. I had been in this position before, and it hadn't turned out well. Trying to rationalize, I couldn't go with my gut or my heart when both were leaning toward the same outcome. It was my history that told me I should say no, but somehow, I had more trust than hesitancy.

I knew he was different. Since I'd been in Austin, Seth had included me anytime he could. Both he and Ben even valued my opinion in the search for a new place to live. He'd said he wanted to get to the good things faster, and I wanted that, too. I transferred the money.

In January, Seth told me he wanted to cross something off his list. He wanted to meet my family. I thought it was a little soon, on top of a little odd, that meeting my family was something to be crossed off some list. I wondered what else was on the list. After coming to terms with the idea being presented, I found there weren't that many reasons not to visit, so we made arrangements.

It was a whirlwind trip but felt great to re-connect with many parts of my family. We headed to Florida to see my sister and daughter then headed to Indiana to see my mom, dad, and two brothers. It had been a long time since I'd seen any of my family, and this time, I was able to bring a serious boyfriend. In the end, I felt that I'd successfully passed a major Seth Stanley test. But...did Seth Stanley pass the test of meeting my family? I also felt proud to achieve such a milestone in my own life.

Over the next few years, I continued to take extended trips to Austin, and for the time I wasn't in Austin, Seth traveled back and forth every three months. We were presented with the reality of both a long-distance relationship as well as living with the other 24/7. I helped Seth move again because the owner of the condo we'd found decided to sell suddenly. Outside of real estate business, he filled our time with zip lining adventures, carriage rides, expensive restaurants, lots of swimming and fantastic shows at the University. I loved every great moment, but ultimately, felt that they were only temporary rushes when all I craved was my simple jungle life.

When Seth was in Hawaii, my free-spirit felt contained, and his presence was in everything I did. On an astrological level, Seth's headstrong, analytical, earthy Taurus wanted to categorize my independent, flirty, head-in-the-clouds double Gemini. When I suddenly had to explain my actions or his anger rose for a reason I couldn't discern, it was like a bull trying to take hold of a butterfly's wings.

I knew I wanted it all. I wanted my freedom to live by my passions, but I also craved that connection with a special someone who'd always be there for me. As opposite as we seemed, I felt Seth was that someone. His quickness to anger had me feeling anxious more than I would have preferred, but I also knew that I needed a strong leader to bring my feet back down to the ground. I kept telling myself this was just one aspect of a bigger picture.

The scales broke one day when Seth became so angry he punched the wall. Like a gag reflex, I vacated my house. I had begun to notice that when Seth could control my time as he did in Austin, we remained balanced, but in Hawaii where my life was solid, he spent more time demanding what I was doing, where I was going, with whom and that he constantly wanted to be by my side. By the time he took the jab at my wall, I had almost completely removed myself emotionally from the relationship, and there was nothing for Seth to do but leave.

The fight or flight phenomenon had become obsolete as my fight was always regurgitated back at me with his skillful words that manipulated my feelings to make my argument a non-issue. Flight became my only option, yet fleeing my own house couldn't continue. Since I had been in abusive relationships before, my past wouldn't let me stay.

In October of 2011, I drove in a silent car for a painful two hours to Kona to drop Seth at the airport. We were heartbroken as we'd both had high hopes for a relationship of a lifetime. It had been the most promising 14 months of my love life, but at the same time, I had felt my sun weaken and flame start to sputter. I cried the whole way back to Pahoa.

Back Together

*A*s much as I was relieved he was gone, I felt doubly lost without Seth. We began emailing, first, as a way to make sure he got back the things he had brought over, then as a way to process our still present emotions. I continued to love him dearly, but I couldn't handle the way he made me feel on a daily basis. We agreed to work on our relationship as we both felt it was worth it. Seth suggested I read a book called *The Five Love Languages* by Gary Chapman.

In the book, Dr. Gary Chapman illustrates what he calls the five love languages. After thirty years of being a marriage counselor, he found five areas, in all marriages, that each partner possesses in varying degrees. After taking the handy test within the book, Seth and I found that we scored similarly in two areas but vastly different in the others. We both needed quality time and physical touch, but I craved kind acts of service whereas Seth needed frequent words of affirmation. The gifts that he had been showering me with were nice but not necessary, and I had never made the extra effort to do more than thank him for something he had done. He needed more cheering and applause when expressing appreciation. He did mention in his Match profile that he was looking for a cheerleader. I had not lived up to what he needed.

In January, Seth returned to Hawaii for another try at a relationship with the improved understanding of our needs. The time we were separated and officially broken up rallied us to tune into each other and communicate more effectively our individual desires. We also agreed to allow space and independence to grow while nurturing togetherness, so we would be stronger as a couple, confident in our own actions, and trusting of the other. It was a mighty task, but we wanted 'us' to work.

And work we did. He understood that when he yelled, I shut down. I finally showed him more appreciation for the hard work he put into everything. It was difficult because we were sometimes painfully aware of our faults as we attempted to do the opposite of our usual patterns. There were times that it all came together, though.

Over the three months that Seth stayed, I had two single campers, and two couples come through Body Temple Bootcamp. Seth added his touch to their experiences and massively upped their transformations. All of the campers raved about what I taught them about fitness and nutrition, but the mindset element that Seth completed made it extraordinary. I had been looking to include this missing link but couldn't figure out how to promote that drive and motivation when everything else said quit. No matter how difficult it was for me to create a space in my life for Seth while still holding onto my independence, I couldn't refute that together; we were an ultimate life-changing duo.

Seth returned to Austin, and six weeks later I joined him. He gave me his old laptop so that I could keep in touch easier. It was lightweight and convenient for travel, so I was very grateful. Since I had a lot of free time and am a little nosy, I poked around the laptop for anything Seth might have left. To my surprise, there was one folder that still contained some files. One was a letter dated March 2010. I opened it up and read a love letter that Seth had sent to me. This one had some minor changes, though, mostly in the way of it *not* being addressed to me.

My heart started racing, and a landslide let loose in my stomach. I first saw Seth's profile in August of 2010, so he had written this months before me. I was devastated. How could he use the same words on two different women? I had been living with him on and off for two years now, and I honestly believed he loved me. Had I just been duped again?

I found this ex-girlfriend on Facebook and scrolled down two years. Sure enough, in April, after the letter had been written, she mentioned that she no longer had a boyfriend. I immediately confronted Seth.

Though he was shocked that I had found the letter, he told me everything. Their relationship had only lasted a year, and it had been spent traveling between Texas and California. Yes, he had loved her once, but their split was mutual, so he claimed, and now, he loved me...lots.

I wondered how he could love so profoundly then let go and find another love so deep in less than six months. The words that I had embraced no longer felt amazing. My head hurt from the anger, frustration, and betrayal. Maddeningly, I still felt a love that beat harder than all the rest of these emotions, yet the letter added to the anxiety I already harbored. He told me to delete it and not hold it against him. I did delete it, but it was etched in my heart.

With our return to the island, we had plenty of fun adventuring, but we kept working diligently on the friction we had. I was still getting used to the fact that I wasn't completely free and did have another person to consider before just taking off. I also had to be conscious of my words, so Seth felt appreciated and not disrespected. Seth had a hard time allowing my independence because he wasn't familiar with Hawaii and felt so protective of me. He'd also had trust issues in previous relationships, so it was difficult to comprehend that I was honest, loyal, and faithful. Like any couple, some days were harder than others, but we tried to maintain a steady course towards a smooth relationship.

Magic Carpet Ride

When Seth went back to Austin in the fall of 2012, it was on very different terms than his departure the year before. Instead of breaking up, we were loving and laughing and working hard at making those moments last longer. In relationships past, I would not have wanted to work so hard at something I thought should have come easy. I accepted that it was a process now and wanted nothing more than to make 'Seth and me' into 'we.'

During his absence this time, I participated in a 30-day appreciation challenge and wrote down ten things every day that made me glad to be alive. It made me realize how much I appreciated Seth. We were thousands of miles apart, but little things would suddenly appear and bring him closer. I sent him songs and wrote little messages whenever I thought of him. It served to bond us together tighter, and when he arrived in Hawaii on December 29th, he brought me two special gifts.

One was a beautifully framed photo of a black sand beach scene with a heart-melting poem he had written. He also gave me a card addressed to "The Love of my Life." Inside, it explained that after I had sent him the song "A Whole New World," from Disney's Aladdin movie, saying that life with him was like a magic carpet ride, he'd figured out what he would give to me for Christmas. Then, it said that we would be leaving on our own magic carpet ride out of Hilo on January 11th, at 7:28 am and outlined a short list of what to bring.

He disclosed nothing more in the days following, but I noticed that he was on the phone being very secretive several times a day. I was a ball of batty energy by the time the day finally arrived despite a tickle of sickness nagging at my throat. At the Hilo airport, Seth still wouldn't divulge any information. In Honolulu, he handed me the next plane ticket which had Kauai printed on it. I was crazy excited.

Landing in Lihue, Seth still kept quiet as I asked, "What's next?" a million times. Standing next to his silence, on an island I'd been wanting to explore for years, drove me nuts. Finally, a car pulls up. The driver rolls down the window and asks, "Harley?"

An hour later, we were streaking down the road on a double seated Harley Heritage. I didn't know where we were going, but I sure as Hell was enjoying the ride! The day just kept getting better. There was a four hour private horseback ride into the mountains, our villa that had a pool and overlooked some ponds by the ocean, a lobster meal at a fancy restaurant where the staff waited on us like royalty, and the evening was topped off with a late night naked popcorn fix.

The next morning, Seth tells me, "Pack some food, wear waterproof, closed toe shoes, pack something nice, and put on a jacket." Again, I had no idea what was in store for us. Moments before, as I hopped on the bike, a sparkle on the ground caught my eye. Stooping down, I picked up a Saint Christopher's medal. Known as the patron saint of travelers, legends paint St. Christopher as a very tall man. He went searching for the greatest king. In his travels, a hermit guided him to serve Christ by using his height and strength to carry travelers across a turbulent river. One day, a child seemed to grow in weight and the river rise as St. Christopher attempted to forge the river. Barely making it, he told the child that carrying the weight of the world couldn't have been heavier. The child replied that St. Christopher had carried the world, and He who had made it, then vanished.

Despite not having firm evidence of his existence anywhere in history, many people today still say a silent prayer to St. Christopher or carry a medal with his visage in their vehicle for protection. The coincidence of being able to pick it up, that morning, and knowing that Seth had very little to no experience with motorcycles didn't escape me. I rubbed the medal, said my silent prayer, and stuck it in my pocket as I climbed on my seat. I set the music in our helmets to the Hawaiian legend of Israel Kamakawiwo'ole and sat back comfortable and fully confident. As the opening bars of "Over the Rainbow" began, the sky gifted us the most magnificent rainbows for our first full day on Kauai.

We rode east toward Waimea Canyon. The views were spectacular with the cerulean ocean and white sand beaches winding up into steep mountain roads and breathtaking canyon views. At one point, I was so overwhelmed I had to close my eyes. The combination of the natural beauty all around us and the love I had for Seth had my adrenaline throatily purring along with the motor. I felt high as a kite, drugged and incapacitated with a euphoria that this was real right now.

Arriving at a rarely used trail, we locked up the bike, stashed the helmets in the trees, and headed out. After two miles of breathtaking scenery, we stopped at a waterfall that emptied into a pool. Hot from the hike, I stripped down to my panties and waded in. Seth followed me and then asked me to sit up on a rock ledge just off of the waterfall. Thinking he was going to take a picture or something, I didn't expect him to wade all the way over to me and start going down on one knee. He took my hand and began a beautiful speech about exploring every rainbow, every waterfall, every mountain and ocean with me for the rest of our lives.

Already blissed out and not believing what he was doing, I kept interrupting. Adding to my absurdity, the tickle in my throat had grown, so my voice was hoarse and cracking as I fumbled around. I wanted to hug him, to hold him, to never have this moment end. Seth kept pushing me back to keep eye contact and finish what he was saying.

It didn't seem real, but I was definitely getting proposed to, in my panties, under a waterfall in Waimea Canyon, on Kauai! Not done, Seth reached under the water into his pocket and brought out a bracelet. Custom made, in silver with a Koa wood inlay, in the shape of Maile leaves, he slipped it onto my wrist as he explained the magic behind it. Maile leaves were used by ancient Hawaiians to bind the wrists of the bride and groom signifying lifelong commitment. The Koa tree is indigenous to Hawaii. It is one of the strongest with some of the most beautiful wood in the world.

Barely able to keep my emotions under control, Seth brought out a second bracelet. This one was also custom made but crafted out of platinum and inlaid with Koa. Made out of the strongest metal and the strongest wood, he said this bracelet illustrated his commitment to our lifelong happiness. He asked me if I would put it on him.

Squeaking and on overload, I threw my arms around Seth. I wanted to say so much, but my thoughts were crushing me. He had just served me a once-upon-a-time magic carpet ride that no one could refuse. I wanted this so much and wanted to scream from the highest mountain how much I loved this man.

Instead, "Okay" was all that came out. I wanted to stop time, so I could make sure this is what I wanted. We weren't perfect, and there were still times that he could squash my soul, but he'd made it plain that I could do the same. We were working so hard to please each other, so why was I suddenly afraid that I was changing? I had visions of nothing but fear emanating from my body. I saw everything that I had worked so hard for taken away because I was too meek to say no, but I also felt what we could be.

Working together, as a team, coordinated in our efforts, we could bring about important transformations for many. This was what I wanted. I wanted to help people. I wanted to share my knowledge. I wanted to live with a man who made life better. Since I'd met Seth, my world had changed. I was so happy. I was old enough to understand that I had to work to get what I wanted. I wanted a forever relationship, so I was sure as Hell going to work for this one.

Goosebumps flashed across my wet body as the spray from the waterfall continued to dance around us, but I was on fire. Seth and I were so close to each other in those moments. Physically kissing, laughing, and caressing each other but also emotionally and spiritually as both our desires were finally coming to fruition. It was indeed a dream come to life.

Hiking back out, Seth said that the magic had only just begun and that we must hurry because we had a date with Honu on the other side of the island. Honu is the Hawaiian word for the green sea turtle. I've always felt strongly toward turtles, so I wondered with anticipation what was up his sleeve. Parking at Hanalei Bay, Seth and I changed out of our sweaty hiking clothes and began walking down the beach.

We came upon the river flowing out of Hanalei Valley, and a green sea kayak sat upon the bank. Seth held out his hand and said, "Meet Honu." He helped me climb in and said we would paddle upriver to the restaurant for dinner. For fifteen minutes, we paddled slowly up the lazy river. As serene and beautiful as it was, I finally had to say, "I think you're mistaken. There's no restaurant." Turning around, Seth mentioned that he'd seen some people on the beach he could ask.

Beaching the kayak, Seth took me with him to ask about the restaurant. As we rounded a little corner, a canopy came into sight. It was fronted by a little bonfire, hung with lights and above a candlelit table set with a white tablecloth, a bottle of red wine and two lei strung with fresh, aromatic, tropical flowers. Two people walked up, warmly greeted Seth and welcomed us for dinner.

By now, my voice was nearly gone, but my body and eyes said it all. His secrecy for the past weeks came into full view. This wasn't ever just a quick trip to Kauai. It was an introduction to Kauai, a trip down memory lane with a private horseback ride, a proposal under a waterfall, and now, a privately catered meal with everything organic or just caught out of the ocean.

Seth led me to my seat as we were served the first course of smoky grilled artichoke and ahi sashimi. A woman with a guitar walked up and began playing Israel's, "On a White Sandy Beach in Hawaii." After the appetizer and a beautiful intermezzo palate cleanser of lilikoi granita with blue curacao drizzle, Seth asked me to dance. In his strong arms with the sand between our toes, under a pink sunset on Hanalei Beach, we were the only ones in existence.

After dinner, satiated with food and love, we intertwined hands and began our trip back to the Harley. Out of the soft lighting of the canopy, the darkness of night enveloped us. Crossing the thigh-high river was cold, yet brought me a real feeling amidst so many I couldn't define. The sand worked our calves but caressed our toes as we stepped in and out of its softness. The ocean roared on our left as it crashed and retreated on the shore. Walking silently and in our reverie, knowing that the day really couldn't get any more perfect, I silently wished to see a shooting star. To me, that would mean my grandparents were looking down on me, rejoicing as well. Sighing with a satisfaction rarely reached, I raised my head into the infinity of space, opening my head and heart to the millions of twinkling stars, and at that moment, a star raced across the sky. It was so clear among the glittering nuances of the night and undoubtedly let me know that blessings had just been given. I yelled to Seth, but in a blink, it was gone. The shooting star was to be mine alone.

The next day we were supposed to go zip lining, but it was raining, and I was so sick that we just spent the morning at our villa. Even the time spent relaxing with my new fiancé and calling family with the good news seemed plush, extravagant, and unbelievable. We took our time on the way to the airport, and we splurged for first class on the way home. The night descended upon us like silk, smooth, luxurious and caressing.

We woke in each other's arms feeling like different people. Our relationship was on another level. I felt a sense of responsibility, purpose, and wholeness. This was a lifetime commitment, and we couldn't have been happier. Smiles weren't enough to convey our elation. Such hard work had preceded this decision and the knowledge that we had so much more ahead of us to accomplish our bigger picture served to cement our commitment. We were both so driven that we knew it was already happening.

Two Weddings

The following months went quickly. For Valentine's Day, we spent the weekend in Kona and picked out custom designs in Koa for our wedding rings. We needed them by July as our wedding was set for early August. Seth and I went back to Austin for another three months, and I tried to stay grounded and sturdy as I reined in my thoughts for our Hawaiian wedding.

Being my third wedding and into my fifties, the last thing I wanted was some over-the-top budget-crushing wedding. Additionally, I heard that most of my family would not be able to make it due to expenses or bad timing, so it didn't carry as much fairy-tale desire as when I was a girl. We wanted to share just how big our love was with our friends and family, but we embraced intimacy to bring balance to our planning.

Knowing how deeply it hurt not to have my family able to attend, Seth presented the idea of a fun, pre-wedding with my family in Indiana. Most of my family was ecstatic and wanted to help in any way they could. My dad and his wife made it clear that they did not like the idea nor did they show any support for us, but they were invited anyway.

In the short time between when the planning began and our arrival in Indiana, my dad sent more nasty, mean, hateful letters to my immediate family members. They carefully illustrated his dislike of his ex-wife and his mother, but the letters didn't leave out his kids either. We were all spurned for our horrible attitudes towards him and his new wife.

They were excruciating to read, so I started to give the un-opened letters to Seth. I still loved my dad and couldn't bear to think that he meant those things. I wondered if he'd changed that much or if his wife was behind it. He was once so loving and supportive. I clung to those memories.

In June, Seth and I left Texas for Indiana. The family fun wedding was set for the 21st. It was Spring Equinox, and I was so excited my feet traveled far ahead of me. Having my mom, both of my brothers, and my sister in the same house, building human pyramids and challenging each other on the four-wheeler, in the yard, was like the past reincarnated. It was incredible being able to include our spouses and children who made it, so wholly in the present, but also to show the next generation how to continue this great family bond.

For a couple of days, we just played. I showed Seth more of my hometown. We spent hours and hours at the country club, and we caught up with so many people from my past. I couldn't have asked for more, and I knew I owed much and more to Seth for it. This wasn't his family, yet he was so willing to arrange it all so that I could be happy. He just wanted to spend the time with me. I was in Heaven, and I wasn't even married yet.

The pre-wedding had everything. After a morning of water-skiing, my daughter Autumn showed up. I hadn't expected her there because she'd planned on being my maid of honor in our Hawaiian wedding. Unbeknownst to me, timing had changed in her life, and she wouldn't be able to make it to Hawaii, so she'd called Seth. They pulled strings so that Autumn could be in this family fun event. She showered me with heartfelt hugs and then told me that I needed a haircut. That was so very Autumn, in style, that it settled many of the unsure feelings between us in the last few years.

My mother and oldest brother walked me down the pier at my brother's house on Lake Freeman though my father was in attendance. My other brother had gotten ordained, over the Internet, so he performed the ceremony. My nephew stood up, as Seth's best man, and my niece's and cousin's young daughter were flower girls. After Seth and I said our vows, my ordained brother, ceremoniously, pushed us into the lake. With music blasting from my brother's boat, we danced on the pier well into the night. As much as I wish my father would have shared a dance with me, there was so much to be thankful for on this day, that I wouldn't allow his disdain to hinder my soaring wings. His refusal sparked a blistering response from a long time family friend who also was there to celebrate with us. She stood up and yelled at my father, "your parents are rolling over in their graves right now at your disrespectful behavior....you should be ashamed of yourself." I looked at him with sad eyes feeling hurt, yet did not allow that to ruin our party.

The wedding for the books back in Hawaii came in a flash. Seth's dad and son were able to come, but the rest of our guests were our beloved friends of Hawaii. Friends from all areas of my life here in Hawaii helped. From flower arranging to catering, video, and photography, Seth and I felt so blessed. Many helped without hesitation. Even the camper staying at Body Temple Boot Camp helped. She had a theater background, so she did my makeup and hair which was great because I've never been good at either.

The day of our wedding we gathered cliffside at Mackenzie State Park. The sun was shining and made a thousand sparkles on the water, glistening and gleaming out the proclamation of our love over and over. Seth's dad walked me through our small group of sweet supporters while Seth's son proudly stood by his dad as best man.

After saying those official words that bound us together, the officiant brought out a stack of papers. She had reached out to my family and asked for a few words of support, encouragement, and tidings of love. What she received was intensely heartfelt letters from my mom, daughter, and sister. I couldn't even get through one before tears were rolling down my face. Unsurprisingly, but increasingly disappointing, my father had been asked but had sent nothing.

The party at the local kava bar was the gala of the summer. Fresh coconuts were cut open and passed out, three bands kept the dance floor hopping, and I seriously felt like a princess. Out of the three weddings in my life, this one was the best. I was more mature than my first, and I wasn't pregnant like my second. This marriage was my choice after all the hard work that Seth and I had put in. Our future held so much promise with the intertwining of talents and love. August 3rd, 2013, we became Mr. and Mrs. Seth Stanley. For the first time in my life, I was the Mrs. I wanted to be.

Teamwork And Triggers

We tried to settle into a routine after the wedding, but it was harder than we expected. Seth was still flying back and forth to Austin every three months so that he could be with his son. He was a devoted dad just as he was showing me every day that he was a devoted husband. Though we were apart for our first Thanksgiving, as husband and wife, I flew to Austin for the Christmas holiday. Knowing that I missed my daughter immensely, Seth arranged privately with Autumn's boyfriend for a quick trip to Atlanta so that I could see her new house.

When we walked in the back door to the new house, we set off a commotion with the dogs. Autumn came down the stairs quickly, and I took her completely by surprise with a, "Hi, honey, we're home and ready for your evening yoga class!" It had been a long time since I'd seen her so stunned, and I'll never forget the look on her face as she came up to hug me. We'd seen each other less than six months before, but the emotion of my unexpected trip made our hug intense. All the years of hoping I'd been a good enough mother, of wishing I'd paid more attention, of having to let her go when I wasn't ready dissipated with every breath we took together. Tears flowed, as words were left unspoken, yet finally understood. Out of all the hugs in my life, I'll never forget this one. It was a full minute of pure, devoted joy.

We got back to the island in January. We were both ready to make progress in business. Seth had been fine-tuning the mindset components for his base camp in preparation for a couple coming in the middle of the month. The company he had been working for was sending them to experience what the camp had to offer, and Seth wanted to make sure everything was lined up.

Three days before the campers showed up, I got a call from my sister. She was in deep trouble. Caught in a downward spiral of addiction, depression, and emotional pain, we'd all known she wasn't well, but until Julie recognized it on her own, there was little we could do. This call was Julie's first step. She said it was the hospital or me and that she'd be here in three days.

A few months earlier, Julie had called late one night. She was drunk and ready to call it quits. She said she'd called our father, begging him to help her. She'd wanted him to reach out to her, to tell her things that he used to say, to let her know that daddy was there to help. Instead, she got silence. No return call, no return text, only silence.

As a big sister, this hurt me just as much as it hurt Julie. To have communication with our once loving father reduced to nasty letters and awkward family moments followed by more vicious unexplained attacks infuriated me. As a mother, I didn't understand how a child's plea for help could go unanswered. As a survivor of bad relationships, I couldn't understand how someone could so poison him that he would abandon his first family or even lose who he was. I lost all respect for him as a father, yet somehow, I didn't want to quit him. I still remembered all the times I looked up at my daddy with love in my eyes. I couldn't just cast him aside.

Seth's campers and Julie arrived hours apart. My sister was the second to come. Seeing how frail and frightened she was, as she walked down the steps of the airport, was hard. I knew she was a survivor. Having battled my own issues, I knew the changes in front of her were going to be tough, yet Julie came here on her terms. She was ready.

Because of the campers, I could not devote 100% of my time to my sister, yet we included her in everything that we could. Seth, knowing how important a step this was for Julie, supported her in every way he could. He helped her with her swimming, and he taught her how to adjust her mindset to one that wanted health. While she was here, she learned all about juicing and how to eat more whole foods that were free of sugars. She was able to wean off of the anti-depressant and sleep aid she'd been prescribed which weren't doing anything except masking her real problems. We ran her and the campers to all of our favorite spots including Uncle Robert's where we'd had our wedding reception, and we taught them the importance of consistency in food and exercise.

The twenty-one days she was here weren't all perfect. Seth's intensity and drive were sometimes hard for Julie to handle since they produced feelings similar to the ones she was trying to escape. One time that Julie pulled me aside, later to discuss, started with a spill in Seth's truck. I immediately grabbed a T-shirt to wipe it up, but Julie felt Seth's mood change and saw that the

T-shirt was not just any T-shirt, but my favorite one. I laughed it off, saying that my favorite shirt could be washed easier than the truck, but she called me on how quickly I'd swept it aside, and how fast I'd jumped to clean it up. Seth also had a heavy conversation with her. She was in a fragile state, but she'd taken steps to get here and to quit now would only make it easier to slip back into exactly what she was trying to overcome.

Hearing the concern of my little sister made me take pause. Seth's flashpoint anger had always been a matter of anxiety, but we'd both been working so hard. I reminded myself that nobody is perfect, and in our most desperate moments, it's hard to remember every aspect we'd learned, so it seemed natural for me to say that it's okay. Besides, when Seth talked about it afterward, there was a definite rationale behind his actions. Quite often, I'd find myself pushing aside my anxiety, in favor of his words, and there was just so much good in between. I was starting to hear things from family and friends, like my sister, saying that I was meek and like a different person around Seth. My mom observed my Spirit was not the same. I wanted this relationship to work so bad that I allowed his magical glossy words to win as I shoved my feelings aside.

After my sister left Hawaii, she returned to her home, joined an AA meeting, let go of many of her toxic friends, and began to work on her marriage. She has been following most of the lessons she learned here for three years now. I am so proud of her time here. Her commitment to herself is the best thing she could have done and to continue, despite many triggers in her life, is a testament to her survival skills.

Broken Wing

2014 was a year of VIP visits, but it also gave us tribulations that had lasting effects.

Just a couple of weeks after my sister left, my mom, brother, and his family came for a vacation. It was the first time any of them had visited Hawaii, so it was special for me to have them see how far I'd come. The week they spent here was bliss, but the hours that happened right before I picked them up were soul crushing.

A couple of hours delayed my family's flight. By the time we got the news, Seth and I were already in town running errands. As we exited the grocery store, I said or did *something* that triggered a sudden, red-hot, anger in Seth. He very loudly told me never to disrespect him. Taken by surprise, I laughed it off and tried to clarify what it was that I did as we got in the truck.

His words quickly became loud and booming, making the cab of the truck intensely claustrophobic. I tried to understand how I'd been disrespectful, but Seth countered with one of his favorite sayings, "Perception is reality." Whatever I'd done, he'd taken personally, and it didn't matter that I didn't know how I'd disrespected him or that he never spelled it out.

In those moments, it seemed as if my reality shifted, and I was suddenly full of fear without knowing the root cause. I knew I couldn't correct it and not knowing how I'd been impertinent; I feared repetition. "Do not ever disrespect me!" Seth roared again, more ferociously than before. With fire in his eyes, he threw the keys at me and told me he'd walk home. Within the hour, I would be picking up my family from the airport.

After he was gone, two ladies in the car next to me asked if I was okay. An employee of the store where we had just bought groceries came out and asked if I wanted her to call the police. Shaken, scared, and still trying to process what had just happened, I thanked them but refused any help. I called Seth on his cell phone and asked, through tears, if he'd come back. I felt his anger was out of the blue and without comprehending what I'd said that he perceived as insolent, this was just added to the pile of unease.

He finally told me where he was, so I went and picked him up. We went to the liquor store without a word and proceeded to the airport where I met my family with flowers in my hand and no tears in my eyes. Seth and I never talked about this fight again though it took two full days for us to return to normal. My supposed disrespect was never defined. There were no apologies, and the whole thing was simply swept under the rug. Despite my surety that Seth was the love of my life, my beautiful butterfly wings got notched that day.

A little over a month after my family left, Seth left to go back to Austin, and my dear friend Kat came to visit for a week. This is the same friend who drove with me across the country when I moved from Indiana to California. Our friendship has always been easy and fun, and this whirlwind week proved no different. I'd set up an apartment area especially for her, but unfamiliar with all of the jungle noises, she didn't even last one night alone, preferring to sleep on the futon within listening distance to me instead.

A week isn't that long to show a best friend all the reasons why you love a place. We stayed close to home, but we tried to hit it all. Time went quickly while happiness reigned supreme. My relationship with Seth had perked up considerably since the fight, but the unrestrained ease that encompassed my friendship with Kat was like the first rush of sunlit air at dawn. I always look forward to time spent with her. We encourage and support each other, and any snags, in attitude, are sure to be followed by warm understanding.

By August, Seth had returned, and a hurricane was set to kiss the shores of Hawaii Island. Thanks to the all of the technology and preparedness of the NOAA and Civil Defense, the residents of Puna were well informed before Hurricane Iselle's landfall, but I don't think any of us were ready for the aftermath.

Natural Disaster

*H*istorically, hurricanes had always skirted the island or been split apart by the mountains of Hawaii Island. Iselle bore down as a Category 1 hurricane without any respite. Seth and I watched on the TV as long as we had power then retreated downstairs with Malia kitty and Gladys, my beloved chicken. Night fell, and the winds picked up speed. Seth laid down to relax and fell asleep not to wake again until morning, but I couldn't find that peace.

In the tornadoes I'd been through in the Midwest, there was always a basement for safe surrender, so I was on high alert above ground amidst the towering trees of the rainforest. All around my house, the trees began to creak and soon crack, as Iselle made landfall less than ten miles away. Technically, she had been downgraded from a hurricane to a tropical storm right before coming into contact with the island, but the few miles difference in wind speed meant little.

Crazy with fear and wonder as the minutes stretched longer, I found myself outside screaming under the bending trees. Suddenly, an explosion from the geothermal plant, less than a mile behind my house, intensified the darkness. The sky lit up red, and I seriously thought we were all going to blow up. Minutes later, trees began falling under the wind's might. Small saplings nicked the house and damaged the corner of the gym, and I watched a huge tree demolish the climbing wall. I was terrified.

When daylight finally came, Seth awoke, and we walked around our property. Leaves and trees littered the ground like a toddler's toys lie scattered in a playroom. Lucky to have minimal damage to the house and gym, the climbing wall was in splinters. We ventured out to the road and found ourselves completely blocked in by massive trees, utility poles, and torn electrical lines swinging freely. We had no power and no water and no way to get out.

After a couple of days, we were finally able to zigzag our way into town, and the reality of rebuilding came full weight upon us. The line for a case of bottled water was two hours long. Some houses, along the shore, had been ripped completely off their foundations. The majority of the district of Puna was without power. Some roads were still impassable, and parts of certain subdivisions were complete disasters. Civil Defense was out in force. The National Guard was deployed. The Red Cross came to help, and the utility companies began assessing the damage.

We also found out that what had sounded like an explosion from the geothermal plant was caused by an emergency shutdown of the plant after the power grid lines to Hilo had gone down which released gasses into the air at a federally accepted level, at least that was the official statement. Anyone who wasn't able to evacuate or shut their windows suffered the aftereffects of inhalation of hydrogen sulfide. We couldn't have gotten out even if we'd heard the evacuation order, so we were two of those affected by harsh eye and throat irritation, coughing and ear pain as well as being lethargic and weak. Some who lived closer had worse symptoms that lasted past the ten to twelve days we had them.

Resilient and full of aloha, many in the community who didn't get as much damage helped in any way they could. Bags of ice from residents' homes were shuttled to those in need. Crock pot meals were given hot and ready to those who lost all of their food. Food stands popped up to give away hot meals, and people with chainsaws worked alongside county and utility workers to cut down trees on roads where people were still trapped. It took twelve days for the electric company to restore electricity fully.

As heavily damaged as the district was, the whole experience reactivated why I'd chosen Pahoa as my home. So many people pitched in to help complete strangers. The spirit of aloha brought the community closer; opposing views were brushed aside to make sure neighbors had food and showers. Even state politicians flew from O'ahu to stand in distribution lines for no reason other than to help. Much of the tropical tree-filled vistas of Puna were blown over in one night, yet the coming together of a community to help those in need was the hug that lifted us.

Not even out of August, the residents of Puna were again greeted by Civil Defense announcements on the radio. This time about lava. Lava is quite literally Hawaii's history, but when intermixed with the magnificent culture, the fiery red liquid rock is transformed into Pele, the Hawaiian goddess of the volcano. Residents of Puna, in the 80's, experienced the powers of Pele when she slowly but devastatingly covered a beloved beach park and swimming hole before entering the nearby subdivision. Some people still vividly remember that. Some, like me, loved that there were times I could easily access the presence of such an intense force of nature but may not have given the current, dependable track into the ocean much thought.

The June 27th flow, as it officially came to be called, exited the Pu'u O'o Crater at a different spot thus falling off the other side of the East Rift Zone and flowing toward the town of Pahoa. Emotions spiked as the flow sometimes advanced 300 feet in a day. Pele's path was erratic, occasionally turning without warning and sometimes heart-wrenchingly slow. Many people moved. Other residents began preparing. Community meetings ran hot, residents fearful and officials unable to predict where the lava would go. Suddenly, we were on the news all over the country.

The Additions

As scary as the thought of lava covering the town I had come to love was, it hadn't happened yet, and the days continued like clockwork whether the lava advanced 10 feet or 300. Not even out of August, I finally decided I'd had enough of the obnoxious renter next door. I did a little investigating and found the owner of the house lived on Kauai and conveniently was a friend of a friend. I wrote a letter illustrating the renter's bad behavior. I was pleased to get an immediate response. In addition to evicting the renter quickly, the owner also wanted to sell the property and asked if we'd be interested.

Ecstatic at the possibilities of expanding the boot camp, Seth, and the woman worked out a deal. Very smoothly, we were owners of two acres. There was much work to be done cleaning up the pig sty the renter left, but the house was solid and would be perfect to house campers in the future.

In addition to expanding our property holdings that fall, Seth and I expanded our family. We picked up a beautiful, sweet half lab, half Border Collie and named her Austin Sprite or simply

Austi. She brought such joy to our lives during this time, and we constantly wondered what we'd done before she joined us.

In November, I prepared to go to Georgia to attend my daughter's wedding. Between funds, our much-loved pets at home, and lava still threatening our town, we couldn't stay for long. Knowing how big this was in my life and for ease of scheduling caretakers, Seth stayed in Hawaii a week longer before coming on a short three day stay for the wedding.

The fairytale wedding that Autumn had planned for came to life. It is not my story to tell though the memories of such pride and accomplishment are. Seeing such maturity exuded from the tiny baby I fought so hard to keep helped me see through the times I felt defeated as a parent. As much as I can feel disappointment in some of my actions through the years, witnessing the strength of the beautiful woman she'd become made me realize I didn't totally fail her. Of course, I'm going to say my daughter truly looked like a princess that day, but she also created a feeling that lasted for days which showed her genuinely humble, beautiful, and silly self. Though I'd met her new husband before, this trip, I was able to spend time with him to see and appreciate all of who he is for her.

It was a wonderful trip, but all too soon I was hugging my daughter goodbye in her bed as I departed early in the morning. Hugging her like this brought back so many memories. When I was finally able to bring her home, I would listen so intently to her baby heartbeat. I thought of the many times I carried her toddler body back to her crib to lay her down again. And, suddenly, she was married. This magical union was spectacular in every way except for the financial burden that fell on my daughter and her new husband. Family members were pitching in to alleviate some of this, and Seth being the good stepdad he was, promised them $2,000 in their planning stages. However, this promise never came to fruition.

Seth and I shared a cab to the airport where we also said our goodbyes. He was to stay in Austin until the new year when he would return to the island. When I got home, the lava flow was still active though it wasn't threatening anything major, life was a little different. Emergency access roads had been built just in case the lava crossed the only highway into town. The rubbish station closed when lava oozed through the fences and burned a neighboring house. Some of the town's businesses also closed while others had lines out the door with people wanting to have dinner in the town before it got taken by lava.

Sentiments ran high, yet there were undercurrents of survival and loyalty as people talked about preparedness.

Take The Stage

*M*eanwhile, I was just anxious to see my Austi bear puppy again. The girl that was home/pet care-taking picked me up at the airport and got me home to our pets. Austi ran down the stairs, at the sound of my voice, and it was non-stop tail wagging and kissing the entire evening. She had also wet the floor and there were poop accidents on the lanai, which meant she was left alone too long. I came to find out that this sweet girl (Michelle) would leave after feeding her in the morning, and not return until late in the day. Austi was 4 1/2 months old, and I felt had been neglected. At least, I was home now and could care for her the way we chose to love and care for our dog. A few weeks after Seth returned, we wanted to take a weekend trip to Kona. It had been two years since our 'magic carpet ride proposal.' We wanted to celebrate and scoot out of chaotic Pahoa with the lava still creeping its way to town.

We ended up taking Austi up to the couple we adopted her from, so she could play with her brother and mother. That worked out well, and it felt great for us to be able to get away and know that she would be cared for and loved. Our Kona trip, as always, was a blast and very rejuvenating for us. We seemed to be humming right along, great, for the most part. Seth was overwhelmed, at times, with generating money to get all bills and debts paid and with creating several new project ideas for our Bootcamp business. He is brilliant, with writing and speaking skills, and a good business coach, yet has a difficult time turning his coaching skills onto himself.

I sensed his frustrations, and he was irritable due to a few stubborn health concerns. He continued to kick ass in the pool, ocean, on the bike, and in the gym - way more than men half his age. I just felt he was having a hard time finding peace within himself, and not only did I sense it, but felt it in his negative, frustrated energy. Also, at this time, I was contacted, via email, by a New York journalist who had read through my website and saw my bio and wanted to come and do a story on me! I was ecstatic and thought, "finally, I can get my amazing, unique story out to inspire, and I hope to help others." I introduced "Annie" to Seth, and a phone call was arranged. For the call, Seth told me to leave and sent me to check on some guys fixing our truck. He did this to monopolize the conversation. When all was said and done, she was no longer coming to do a story on me, but now the story would be about *Seth's* BaseCamp. He was once again in control and getting the spotlight.

I felt robbed and jealous on the one hand, yet happy for him on the other. He so deserved the recognition he craves and a story on what he is offering. He loves the acknowledgment and attention, and all I wanted was to have fun with this new woman and teach/share what I could. I was a pouting baby for several days, but when it came down to it, I was quite happy Annie was coming here, and we were going to share what both of us had to offer as a team. Where else can you go to have a dynamic, nationally ranked athlete couple, with entirely different backgrounds, and so much to offer, serve and teach you, guide you on amazing adventures in paradise, train you, and kick your ass? And, you get to do it inside and outside of a unique gym, in the jungle. And, you feast on an organic retro raw regenerative diet? Again, where can you go for this experience? Nowhere! There is no place on this planet like this, and no one offers what we do here.

When this cool, little journalist chick arrived, and we got into our groove, everything went better than great, and we all worked well together just as we had done in the past. I just needed to work through my hurt feelings which did cause friction, and I felt bad after. Much later, I would come to understand that is is part of the cycle of living in a relationship with a narcissistic sociopath.

By the time Annie, the journalist, arrived, the lava flow had come to a stop. She was here for five of the most beautiful days of weather in some time, and on the day she left, it started to rain. It continued to rain, on and off for two weeks, which was so needed and welcomed due to our hot, dry winter weather. Aside from the damn geothermal plant just behind us which we will continue to fight, life is incredible, and we welcome those who want and desire a transformation, or perhaps, to even reinvent themselves, in any way. This was the message that we had shared with Annie.

We also sought to impart to Annie that the new diet, life-style and life plan, change in mindset, a new level of fitness and more will continue to be etched in, deeper and deeper, as you ultimately reinvent your self into the person you want to be. Live your dream, and you can start the process. Look at what all I have experienced and lived through only to come out a better person with a vision and purpose. Let me help you to do the same, no matter what your past or history is. This does not define your future. This was the Body Temple Boot Camp's message. Annie left knowing my personal mission. It is the same mission I passionately live and share with my campers to this day.

Between the time Annie left, and the end of 2015, my relationship...my marriage with Seth blew up and ended.

Fear Can Kill

The last part of 2015 was by far the lowest, most challenging, hurtful, depressing, yet eye-opening time of my life. Would I crumble and fade away to nothing, devastated by the pain of truth, or would I welcome this with the mindset that it is my great opportunity to learn, grow, and finally realize a lesson that has been presented time and time again to me throughout my life?! Is this the reason Grandfather had "sent him to me" to make sure I would learn and not continue to repeat heart crushing lessons over and over throughout time?

Middle of June 2015, Seth moved here full time, after four years of back and forth travel to Texas every three months. This worked out well for us, especially me, since during his time away I could regain a bit of my freedom to go and do as I wanted, say and behave as my spirit desired which was nothing other than loving, fun, and playful. During those three months, I did miss him, and the close, loving moments we did share and the security I felt with him.

When Seth arrived at the Hilo airport in June, and knowing his entire materialistic life was on a boat being shipped to Hawaii,

I admit I felt excited to see him and have him back but anxious that I was going to be unable to be and say what he wanted and needed for him to be happy. Also, knowing that the stressful times we did experience would not go away because he was in Hawaii for good, were a concern. I felt his happiness revolved around me and my ability to be what he needed me to be for him…his cheerleader, his motivator, his lover, his perfect wife.

Tensions rose when we began construction and making improvements to both the main house (my house) and the dolphin house (cabin next door) he purchased. Money was being spent that we did not have, and the debts were growing. I, personally, would not have taken out more loans or charged up more on my card when the income was not there to support it, but I trusted Seth and his word that he could and would pay for all. When all of his things arrived, it was quite a trick trying to find space and make room for all of the stuff. He and a friend did do a good job building a tool room and creating a storage area for all of his REI camping gear. I mean LOADS of stuff.

I somewhat removed myself from all that was going on and left it up to the boys to figure out. I noticed when I did not give enough positive pats on the back and vocalize appreciation more than once or twice a day, it just was not enough, and I could feel the irritation and the yelling began. Again, this time more frequently, louder, and more hurtful words screamed at me, to the point, I was in fight or flight mode quite often and became fearful of him.

I would shut down and not talk much for fear of saying the wrong thing leading to a fight, but my shutting down is what triggered his anger, and the yelling continued, especially in the evenings when alcohol was involved. I could not be who he wanted me to be. I communicated with my heart and emotions, and he straight from the head. I began to feel stupid and like something was wrong with me. I felt the life start to go out of me and my sparky flame begin to become dim light.

In August, I went to see my ND, and she performed some lab tests. When they came back, she called me in and was quite worried about what they showed. She was also concerned about my weight loss and the fact that I just seemed low and unhappy. She explained I was in a highly, dangerously, oxidative state. It was killing me. She explained it by saying my labs showed that I was living in a constant state of fight or flight (panic mode) and something had to change fast. She suggested Seth and I separate for a bit, and I (or we) seek counseling.

I agreed to see her therapist, on staff, but Seth said no way to separation...might as well get divorced, he felt. He also yelled at me that he did not need therapy. He said he had done a lifetime of self-improvement and read all of the books..."how many books have YOU read," he screamed at me. Again, I felt low and stupid. I just said sometimes it takes more than books and an actual person to talk with can help. He said he could talk circles around any therapist.

I showed up to my first therapy session shaking and very nervous. I had turned into a bundle of nerves and lost my confidence. A tall, beautiful woman with long, grey-blond hair came out for me and hugged me. I felt peace and acceptance and willing to share my feelings knowing she would not judge me. This was the beginning of the most difficult and hurtful, yet empowering and regaining time, of my life.

It was only two sessions before Gail looked at me seriously and asked "how long are you going to live like this?" and "do you want to stay in this abusive relationship?" I told her I did not want to quit and that I loved Seth and wanted to try but could make no promises. She said she needed to see us both if I was ready for that. I said okay, and Seth agreed to come after he met with her alone. He said if it took counseling to save the marriage, he would go and give it a try.

Our session together was difficult, to say the least. I nearly threw up with anxiety. We each had our assignments to make lists of what attracted us to the other person. Then, we had to share and not speak to one another but only through Gail. Bottom line: Seth wanted a promise that my commitment to wanting our marriage to work would mean that no matter what, we do not break up, and we make it work. I committed to trying my best but could not promise or guarantee anything. I needed to feel like I could just be me, and be loved for that...not yelled at or looked at with eyes that could kill any longer.

Seth and I both continued to see Gail separately, for weeks, but the yelling did not stop. On a counseling session done down at the warm ponds, Gail again asked how long I am going to do this. Seth is Seth, and he is not going to change. He feels he has done no wrong. We are two very different people and not good for one another. I cried. I could not do it any longer. I was crumbling. I told her I could not tell him alone. I was afraid. She agreed to stay with me. After sending him a text, we would all talk in Seth's office. Gail and I came back to my house, and we met with Seth in the cabin office. He raised his voice, and I started to shake. I was so conditioned to fear him when his voice got loud. Gail was the buffer, and our talk ended peacefully, yet Seth and I were still in a state of 'nowhere land.' I was afraid to lose him, yet terrified to stay with him. That night was the hugest yelling we had, and I wanted to run away. Seth screamed, cussed, and threw his glass of vodka. I decided that was God's message to me that it was time to end it. So, I did.

The next few months were a living Hell as Seth angrily moved out and into his cabin house just next door. Countless texts and emails came which only buried me deeper into my depression.

I was strongly encouraged by family and friends to get a good attorney to get this over with and stop communications with Seth. He was a master with words and knew how to push my heart buttons and manipulate me into believing and doing what he said. I continued to lose weight, cried, and felt sick daily. Only after receiving a phone call offering much information about the man I thought I knew, did I know I was doing the best thing and to continue with the most bad ass attorney I could find. Thanks to a loving family member, I was able to get a decent old car for transportation and get my shark attorney retained.

Learning that Seth had another previous wife that he neglected to mention was just the beginning of the hurtful, deceiving information given to me, leaving me with the feeling that I was never truly loved, only a possession and my whole life with Seth was an illusion I created. Reality and truths crushed and shattered this illusion along with my heart.

I was told to watch my wallet as he had left a string of people in debt and to change my locks and passcodes on everything. The 'do not trust him' thing, and 'be very careful part' scared me even more. I felt like I had been sleeping with the enemy, and now he was a stone throw away. I saw him every day, and we shared a dog and her care.

My counselor encouraged me to dissolve this marriage, and my attorney labeled him a parasite. I blamed my self for letting such a man manipulate my mind and my heart.

I met with my attorney several times, papers were filled out, signed, and turned into the court. Seth was served, and his 'war' began. In-between all of his mean texts and emails, he retained an attorney. Several divorce decrees were drawn up and sent before one was finally agreed upon, only after the wording was changed per insistence of Seth. My attorney was done messing around and said, "this is it, or we see you in court." A final draft was finally signed. All documents were sent to the judge to sign and declare us legally divorced on December 31st, 2015.

My granddaughter was born premature, but healthy, on the 29th of December marking a new life, a new beginning...for both of us...the new baby and her "Tutu" would start a new life.

Moving On

Time to change my story, my patterns that have not served my higher purpose. My hearts desires and my inner voice shall be my guides. My wishes have become clear visions that will come to fruition. I have intention. I have the will. I alone possess the power to do this.

I live simply and humbly, in a jungle, on an island, yet I see clearly into the separating clouds a sparkly castle full of everything I want and deserve. I see a beautiful fairy princess ready to grant wishes, and all I have to do is will all I so desire to me...out of the castle, in the clouds, down into my *real* world, and life in the jungle paradise.

It is time. Previous chapters of my life are closed and done leaving me only with the gifts, lessons, and tools to move forward with confidence leaving all pain, hurts, and regrets behind. And forgiving, not only those that I allowed to hurt me, but also my self, for not listening to my *inner* voice when it was there all along and for how I dealt with many of my pains and may have, in turn, hurt others.

Eight months after my separating from Seth, I had a 90-minute "soul reading" from an amazing teacher, Toby. He reminded me just how very powerful I am and how very important it is to start an all-new chapter in my life. This chapter brings me the best yet. As I open up and receive my wealth from a prosperous purposed life, I will receive a much desired and deserved healthy, honest, happy, loving relationship. I now realize the tapestry of my life is so unique and beautiful. Even the grey threads are beautiful and important because, without them, I would not be who I am today. Yes, I *am* grateful for all of my difficult, challenging, hurtful experiences.

Toby took me to what I felt to be a womb-like cave which was a BIG lava tube by the ocean with a yoni...yes, a vagina-shaped formation, right in the middle about 15 feet long. The cave was around 100 feet long full of lava boulders to climb up and over. I envisioned this to be a birthing canal. It was no cake walk to get through. Vines hung from the top, and there was water dripping from condensation. It was darker than dark, with the only sound being the drips of water, reminding me I was not just floating in the abyss.

We took offerings and were clear about our intentions. Toby channeled a bit as he was being told by my Spirit counsel to speak to me for them. Their message to me: I hold great power to change many lives. Abundance and wealth will come to me as I, full throttle, move ahead to live my purpose with passion, on a much larger scale, than my occasional local clients. No more looking back, and if I find myself doing so or get stuck, I am to look in the mirror and see just how much power I have within and remember my purpose. Now, I do a ten-minute meditation every day to fill me up with violet light then shield myself from hurt. In so doing, I ground myself.

I also imagine a violet, loving light around those that have hurt me and send them love and compassion. If it is too difficult to do seeing them as an adult, then I just imagine them as a hurting little child. I do this practice daily with the two men that were a big part of my life yet were the source of much pain. I do hope the love I send to them penetrates their shell, and they feel it.

Paradoxically, the very place I'd been running from much of my life was now the place I am running to...back to my Self where true happiness and pure joy and my full power on switch is found.

When I reconnected to the parts of me that I had lost to feelings of imprisonment or fear, it felt like a coming home. I have learned that true self-love is when we come home to ourselves...return to our "Source." This relationship which I was unconsciously running from or trying to destroy, during parts of my life, has turned out to be *the* relationship that not only would save my life but be where my source of pure positive, loving power to achieve or manifest *anything* lies. In this space, I, ultimately, not only can love, and help my Self but any others ready to do the work and receive.

I see so many people addicted to behaviors, food, substances, and external relationships, believing or feeling they cannot stop or break free...or maybe, even that they need these things to live. In reality, these are the chains keeping us from truly finding and knowing ourselves where our true source of joy and power lie.

Embrace life, be present, be mindful, and don't stay in your 'problems.' Allow your feelings to live. Then, let go and move on.

You cannot run fast enough to escape them. Your freedom, power, and bliss are found in breaking your chains and living in the *now*. The magic that is found there is immeasurable.

I have mastered the art of chain breaking time and time again only to find myself imprisoned again. I believe I have finally cracked the code to this pattern. Maybe, it was the timing. Maybe, it is in living in a magical place surrounded by such powerful mana, supportive, understanding, loving, friends and family. Maybe it was crawling through this last monstrous, crushing, hurtful phase that I have finally been able to recognize my patterns and developed the ability, confidence, and inner power to break out and fully let go and trust in and love myself.

I now feel grateful for all of my past experiences. For without them, I may have never reached this point…this destination…me fully and joyfully returning *freely* HOME!

Epilogue

Now over four years have passed since my father has spoken to or even acknowledged me. He has dismissed his children and grandchildren and never acknowledged his new great-granddaughter. I still miss him terribly.

Maybe best to just "leave it alone" and let him live with his decisions, but there will always be a part of me that wonders... what if I tried even harder to have him back?

My sister continues to be free of alcohol and drugs, eats a more nutritious, healthy diet, and exercises regularly. She also has a new positive group of friends.

My daughter, Autumn, her hubby, their pups and the newest addition, now a toddler daughter, Emmy, are joyful, healthy, and happy.

My mom, brothers, and families are all well, happy, and healthy back in Indiana.

Shortly after our divorce, Seth moved in with another woman on the Mainland far from his once home in Hawaii.

Living on eggshells sucks the life out of you.

When a butterfly loses the color from her wings, from the gusting hurricane of hate, she shall lose her destined flight in life and just hover above the ground, always in reach of the hand of control.

A note I had written to myself while writing this book: Teach your children to be somewhat tough...to speak up when something does not feel 'right,' to question things, and not just take at face value. Have a voice and use it. When I was young, we were taught to listen to adults, show respect, and for the most part, do what they say...they know best. Teach your children to be bold, yet remain respectful. Adults do not know everything, and not all adults are good people. Teach them to respect their own bodies, hearts, and minds and not to allow anyone to abuse or hurt them.

A quote written for me by a supportive friend: "the greatest victory is thriving in light of someone who has hurt you."

Learn from your experiences and look at them as a gift and not a curse. Learn from your past. Then, let it go. (Hapai is the Hawaiian word for this)

Do not remain the rock stuck in painful memories and patterns. Be the butterfly, and set yourself free. Live in the now and with Faith in the future.

Forgiveness is huge, and appreciation can set your attitude. Create your own memories, and live life on your own terms. Always be true to yourself and "Live Love."

Never waste a moment of your time.

Finally, and most importantly, I am back to living life MY way and will always and forever continue to do so no matter what.

Life is precious, and when you find what your gift or gifts are, realize your purpose by giving them away! I will always be true to my self now and never give my zest for life away. My heart may love again, and I hope it does, but for now, I am feeling very protective of it. I rejoice in serving others, and I am so blessed to have found my ability to now listen to my "Na'au" (inner or God voice) and not just act with my heart or emotions.

In closing, I must share the story of my name. The name "Kieba" was bestowed to me by a client at Frogs Athletic Club in Encinitas California over 15 years ago. She said I was like a sunrise to her - always bright and cheery bringing in every day with a sense of newness and lighting up myself and those around me. She said where she came from, the street names were Native American Indian words and Koba meant sunset and is what she named her dog. She explained that Kieba meant SunRise and is a better name for me. Being that my birth name is Dawn, and my daughter was going to be leaving soon to start her own life, apart from me, I felt a new name that meant a new beginning was suitable. I have been Kieba ever since that day.

ALOHA, SHAKA, and NAMASTE to all.

Meet Kieba

At 31 years old, bulked up and strong, just before dieting
for a contest. Taken where I was living at the time.

At 33 years old, leaned out and show ready for Nationals.

Just won the California championships, and my daughter runs on stage and jumps into my arms!

This baby and I made a deal to gain weight and be healthy,
and we both did.

My sweet daughter and her little family.

A recent picture:
happy, healthy, and living my purpose with passion.

About The Author

Kieba Blacklidge is the owner of Body Temple Boot Camp, a jungle oasis, in Hawaii, where she hosts campers from all over the world and teaches them about fitness, healthy eating, and mindfulness as well as exploring the natural wonders of the area and leading all types of outdoor adventures. Kieba lives in joy and seeks to impart an *everything is possible* mindset to her guests. Her pedigree includes teaching special needs children and being a world-class athlete and bodybuilder. She loves sharing her knowledge as a fitness coach and her skills making food both healthy and delicious with others.

To learn more about Kieba, please visit www.bodytempleboot camp.com

88061499R00135

Made in the USA
Columbia, SC
31 January 2018